Old HAWICK

with ADDERSTONSHIELS, APPLETREEHALL, ASHKIRK, BEDRULE, BONCHESTER BRIDGE, CHESTERS, DENHOLM, HOBKIRK, MINTO, MOSSPAUL, ROBERTON, STOBS and TEVIOTHEAD

Alex F. Young

Stenlake Publishing Ltd.
2004

ORTH END, HAWICK 3938

ISBN 1 84033 295 6

**The publishers regret that they cannot supply
copies of any pictures featured in this book.**

FURTHER READING

The books listed below were used by the author during his research. Only one is available from Stenlake Publishing. Those interested in finding out more are advised to contact their local bookshop or reference library.

Dan Buglass, *Ken Oliver: The Benign Bishop*, Marlborough/ Punchestown, 1994.

Dr D.W. Cameron, *The First Hundred Years (1885–1985), History of Hawick Cottage Hospital*, 1985.

John L. Coltman, *First Hundred Years, Teviotdale Harriers Club, 1889–1989*, Teviotdale Harriers Centenary Committee, 1988.

Owen Connelly, *Seven Score Years*, Hawick Saxhorn Band, 1995.

James Edgar, *History of Lodge St James, B.U.R.A., No. 424, Hawick*, 1932.

Edgar's Hawick Guide, Directory, and Year Book, 1906.

Francis H. Groome, *Ordnance Gazetteer of Scotland*, Thomas C. Jack, Grange Publishing Works, Edinburgh, 1886.

Margaret Sellar, *Denholm: A History of the Village*, Margaret Sellar, 1989.

R.E. Scott, *Companion to Hawick and District*, Deans & Simpson, 1970.

W.A.C. Smith, *The Borders' Last Days of Steam*, Stenlake Publishing Ltd., 2002.

Charles A. Strang, *Borders & Berwick: An Illustrated Architectural Guide*, The Rutland Press, 1994.

Memories of a Great Club, PSA (RFC), 1919–1994, 75th anniversary brochure.

ACKNOWLEDGEMENTS

The author would like to thank the following for their assistance during his research: John Allan, Ian Anderson, Mary Anderson, Kenneth Brisbane, Alex Burgon, Jim Coltman, John L. Coltman, Sam Corbett, Lorraine Cureton, Jane Currie, John Davidson, Elizabeth Donnan, Pat Douglas, Dave Easton, Sandy Fleming, Joe Galletta, David Gaylor, Basil Gray, Robert Grieves, Dr Eric Hillerton, Betty Hopkins, Alan Inglis, the Rev. Anthony Jones, Peter Little, James A. Mackay, Ann McCombe, Gordon McDonald, Cormack McMichan, John Morran, John Paxton, Denholm Reid, Alex Renwick, Mary Rettie, Trevor Skelton, David Stewart, Kathleen W. Stewart, Bill Thomson, Jean Wintrope, Zilla Oddy and Richard White (Hawick Museum), Brian Emmerson (Hawick Saxhorn Band), A.R. Renwick (Hawick PSA Rugby Football Club), Isobel Chlopas (Teviotdale Harriers Club), Captain James Sabiston (Hawick Salvation Army), Moira Sinclair (Teviothead School), Drumlanrig Primary School, Alloa Library, Carlisle Library, Hawick Library, Scottish Borders Archive and Local History Centre, Selkirk, Sandra Reid (Parks & Cemeteries, Hawick), Chris Sullivan (Prudential plc), Timothy Neal (National Fairground Archive, Sheffield University), Ian McCutcheon, and Catherine McLaughlin (Milk Development Council). The publishers wish to thank Jean and Mark Tait for contributing most of the photographs in this book and Robert Grieves for the upper photograph on page 10.

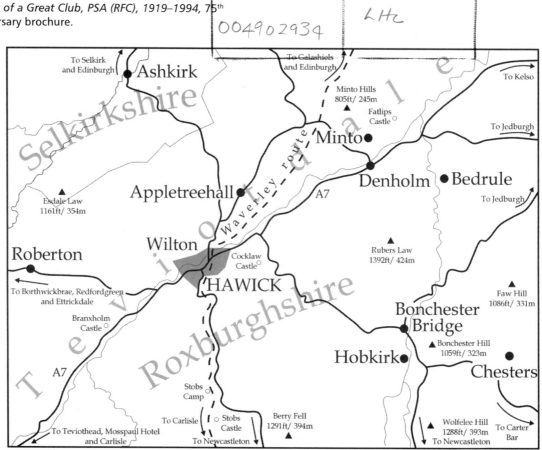

Introduction

Deriving its name from either the Old English *haga wic* ('a settlement surrounded by a hedge') or the Celtic *ha* ('a mansion') and *wic* ('the crook or confluence of rivers'), Hawick is first recorded in the *Chronicle of Melrose* where the consecration of the Church of St Mary by the Bishop of Caithness in 1214 is noted. (The church was rebuilt in 1763 and underwent extensive restoration after a fire in 1880.) The founding of a church would suggest that a settlement had already been established and Hawick is named on the Gough map of the mid-thirteenth century and was a settlement of sufficient size and importance to be noted on Pont's map of 1600. Standing on the south bank of the confluence of the River Teviot and the Slitrig Water, Hawick was then a separate parish and community from Wilton, 'the farm by the willows' on the north bank of the 'sweet and silvery Teviot'. In 1861 the Burgh of Hawick was extended to include Wilton.

The Scottish Rolls of 1347 record Hawick as a settlement owned by the descendants of Richard Lovel of Castlecary and Hawick (d. 1253), having been in his family's hands from 'time immemorial'. It was a burgh of regality by 1357. For a time, through the hand of King David II (1324–71), it was held by Maurice de Moravia, before passing to Sir William Douglas, 1st Earl of Drumlanrig (d. 1427), through a charter granted by King James I (1394–1437). It became a burgh of barony in 1511. Parts of this period of the town's history are still incomplete (there is reference to early documents 'lost and destroyed, during the inroads of the English plunderers' made in the 1790s *Statistical Account*). The 1537 charter, granted by Sir James Douglas, 7th Earl of Drumlanrig (1498–1578), confirming its status as a burgh of barony, was endorsed in May 1545 by the two-year-old Queen Mary (1542–87).

The town had at that time 110 houses – including the manor house, church and mill. Later, to manage its affairs, a town council of 31 was appointed. This consisted of two bailies and a council of fifteen (all appointed for life) with two 'quartermasters' (officials) from each of the seven trades – weavers, tailors, hammermen, skinners, fleshers, shoemakers and baxters (bakers). The town clerk was chosen annually. This form of local government continued until 1861 when a new municipal constitution introduced a council of provost, with four bailies and twelve councillors who were also police commissioners. In 1867 the town acquired the rank of parliamentary burgh, uniting with Selkirk and Galashiels to send the Right Hon. George Otto Trevelyan to Westminster.

Scotland's first census, showing its population to be 1,265,000, was undertaken in 1755. Hawick parish then had 2,713 inhabitants. As part of his work for the 1790s *Statistical Account*, the Rev. Robert Gillan found the figure had increased to 2,928 – comprising 1,378 males and 1,550 females, with 2,320 in the town and 608 in the countryside. By 1838 this had increased again, to 5,308 in the town and 692 in the rural area.

As eighteenth century Britain drifted into industrialisation, Hawick capitalized on its natural resources – the surrounding hills for sheep and the rivers for power. As early as the 1640s there are references to the 'wabsters' or weavers and by 1669, despite poor communications – there was a road to Ashkirk and Selkirk but mere tracks, or drover's roads, to Langholm and Jedburgh – the town had an active market. Communications improved with the introduction of the turnpike road system, opening to Langholm in 1764 and to Kelso, Selkirk and the Carter Bar in 1768, and a weekly carrier service to Edinburgh, Glasgow, Carlisle, Newcastle and Berwick was established.

Subsidised by the Board of Trustees for Improvements and Manufactures in Scotland, William Robertson's 1758 carpet mill was soon followed by other small mills producing serges for carpets and rugs and table covers. By 1780 a stocking manufactory, started in 1771 by Bailie John Hardie with four hand looms, was in the hands of John Nixon who, in the 1790s, employed 42 spinners and thirteen framework knitters, producing annually 3,505 pairs of non-bespoke white and coloured lambs' wool hose. In 1804 Nixon opened the Lynwood yarn and carding mill and William Wilson, who had started in 1788 as a framework hosiery knitter, became the first to convert to steam power. In partnership with William Watson & Son, their 1812 output amounted to 45,000 lbs of yarn and over 50,000 pairs of hose. In 1783 the manufacture of 'inkle' (broad linen tape) began, but it is not clear whether the flax was produced locally or imported. By 1797 the textile industry was employing 362, including the 'cottage' side, where women, supervised by manufacturers' agents, worked in their homes.

Around 1810 Dickson's & Laing's mill was established (introducing power looms in 1830), and in 1815 John and Robert Pringle were established. By the late 1830s there were eleven large-scale mills, including one that was steam driven, and the industry employed 1,788 operatives working 1,209 stocking frames to produce over one million pairs while 226 weaving looms turned out over 12,000 items of underclothing. From 1830, with the opening of the gasworks, much of this work was done by gaslight. The dust-laden atmosphere of the mills may have encouraged the opening of a brewery in 1825 to serve some 53 inns and grocers, but the Rev J.A. Wallace thought, 'it is not to be doubted that these have exerted a prejudicial influence on the morals of the people.'

In the midst of this apparently industrialised wasteland was one oasis – Dickson's nursery. Founded at Hassendean Burn in 1729, the company came to a 39-acre site in Hawick where a workforce of up to 50 raised trees, both forest and fruit, and flowering plants and shrubs for a market encompassing the south of Scotland and England as far as north Wales. They were later superseded by John Forbes whose eventual market covered the globe.

The opening of the railway line from Edinburgh in 1849 – and its continuance to Carlisle in 1862 – opened a new era of prosperity which included the establishment of the *Hawick Advertiser* (1854), the Archaeological Society (1856), a sewerage system (1875), the golf club (1877), a new town hall (1884), and the Co-operative Society (1885/86). In the 30 years from 1861, the population rose from 8,191 to 19,000, but a decade later had dropped to 17,000. However, an extensive house-building programme was implemented around Myreslaw Green, the Wellington Street and Dickson Street areas, Mansfield, and the Earl Street area.

The twentieth century brought the mills their ups and their downs. The declining popularity of woollen underwear was compensated by the rising popularity of the luxury trade in pullovers (started by Henderson's around 1905) and cardigans, but it was hit by the Depression and by 1932 unemployment stood at 1,600 – five times the 1927 figure.

Somehow the industry struggled through the remainder of the 1930s, the Second World War and into the '50s, but the tide of imported, cheaper, textiles was making its presence felt. Closures and takeovers were starting to increase. In 1964

Wolsey took over Lyle & Scott and Renwick's went to Jaeger. Pringle of Scotland, for a time Britain's third largest knitwear business, with 2,000 employees and a factory in Berwick, was taken over by the Dawson Group in 1967. Although many more changes, closures and takeovers were to come, in retrospect these have left a leaner and fitter industry.

The closure of the Waverley Line in January 1969, amidst loud protest, was the end of an other era, but looking today at the Teviot Leisure Centre and the grass swards around it, it is hard to imagine it was ever there. There is the promise of the railway reopening – but don't call Scotrail for a timetable, just yet.

Opposite: The town viewed from Duke's Wood (named after the Duke of Buccleuch) around 1908. On the left of the photograph is the Slitrig Water with St Mary's Church and the town hall standing above. To the left of the river is St Cuthbert's Church manse (then occupied by the Rev. E.T.S. Reid), with the 1858-built church beyond. In the centre is the road to Newcastleton (now Liddesdale Road) and to the right of that stands St Cuthbert's School and William Elliot & Sons' Stonefield Mill (built c.1850 and, at its height, employing 332 spinners).

THE COMMON RIDING

With the Common Riding forming not only a large part of this book, but a large part in the life of Hawick, a brief outline of the event would not be out of place here.

Its roots lie in the ancient annual ceremony, held on the last Friday in May (old style calendar), of marking the boundaries of the town's common land by 'Riding the Marches' and making a formal declaration of the town's legal rights to these boundaries, and also a celebration of the Callants, i.e. the youth, of the town seizing the English pennant during a skirmish at Hornshole shortly after the disastrous Battle of Flodden in 1514. The day moved from May into June when Britain finally adopted the Gregorian Calendar in 1752.

Hawick's first Common Riding is not recorded, but was probably contemporary with Selkirk's, recorded in their Burgh Court Books as happening in 1530. From the *Annals of Hawick* we learn the first known Cornet was in 1703: 'May 17 – The said day the Common-Rydeing was ordained to be upon Fryday the twenty-eight of May, James Scott, called Laird, was voted to carry the pencell.'

The Cornet is chosen in early May, when the Provost's Council, on the recommendation of the two previous Cornets (the Right and Left Hand Man to be), nominate a suitable young man who must be an unmarried 'Teri' (a native or inhabitant of Hawick) planning bachelorhood for at least two years.

On the following Tuesdays and Saturdays in May the Cornet and his equestrian supporters visit the surrounding villages and, on the Thursday evening preceding Common Riding week, visit St Leonards to formally order the 'Curds and Cream' refreshment to be taken after the Common Riding Friday morning Chase. The Chase represents the capture of the English pennant.

The week proper starts on the Sunday morning with the walk to the church for the 'Kirkin' o' the Cornet' service and, later in the day, the laying of wreaths at the Hornshole Memorial. On the following mornings the Cornet and his entourage ride out to St Leonards, the Cornet carrying the 'Blue Banner' on the Thursday.

On the Thursday evening, 'The Nicht Afore the Morn', the 'Colour-Bussing' ceremony is held in the Town Hall, with the Cornet's Lass presenting the Flag to the Provost who, in turn, puts it into the safe hands of the Cornet who is charged with returning it 'unsullied and unstained' after riding the Common next day.

The Friday is Common Riding Day, and proceedings start with the Drum and Fife Band arousing the town for the 6.00 a.m. 'Snuffin'' ceremony, where snuff is dispensed to the crowd from a large horn at St Mary's Church. Such is the pushing and jostling, particularly for the prized packets of snuff thrown into the crowd, that some, unkindly, have likened it to a melee.

The Cornet and his supporters (the Right and Left Hand Men, and Acting Father) then retire to a hostelry for breakfast, and the Provost with his colleagues and guests to the town hall. When they reassemble, it is to parade around the town before setting out towards Nipknowes for the main Chase.

As a prelude to the Chase, the Acting Father and the married supporters gallop up the hill, before the Cornet, grasping the Flag, follows with the unmarried supporters. Then, with the Flag in the safe hands of the Acting Father, all retire to St Leonards for the Curds and Cream repast at the Hut.

Mounted again, it's off by way of Williestruther Loch and Acreknowe Reservoir to 'Ride the Marches' to the end of the Common, where the Cornet 'Cuts the Sod', marking the ancient boundary.

At the racecourse, with the Flag on the roof of the committee room, the Cornet rides the course and is presented with a riding crop as a memento of his day. Following round Crumhaughhill and Myreslawgreen they come to the Coble Pool on the Teviot, where the boundary is marked by lowering the flagstaff thrice into the water. Returning to the town hall the Flag is displayed from the balcony. The day ends with the Dinner, where the Cornet is presented with his Medal, and the Ball with dancing until dawn, which is greeted from the summit of the Moat.

The festival closes on the Saturday with a wreath-laying ceremony at the War Memorial in Wilton Lodge Park, an afternoon's racing on the Moor, and the return of the Flag to the provost.

Prominent on the left of this 1925 view of High Street, fourth building down, is the Venetian style frontage of the 1863-built British Linen Bank (later Bank of Scotland) with the equally grandiose premises of its competitor, the Royal Bank of Scotland, opposite (seventh down from the right, this was built in 1859 by the Edinburgh architects Peddie & Kinnear). The Royal Bank later moved to the old National Bank of Scotland building at 33–35 High Street. Beyond the British Linen Bank is a sign for the dentist William Edwards who was succeeded by Grace Dick.

High Street, photographed around 1912. Under the pestle and mortar, at number seventeen, are the premises of John Craig, the chemist and aerated-water manufacturer who came from Darvel in Ayrshire. Next door are the premises of Thomas Scott the tobacconist and fishing-tackle dealer, then John Riddle's butcher's and John Park's drapery, toymaker's, fancy goods merchant's, and – as can be seen from the Anchor Line advertisement – shipping agent's. This business was founded in 1831 by David S. Park, who was born at Abertay, Inverness, in 1807.

The Crown Hotel at 22 High Street, photographed around 1910 with, perhaps, William Kennedy, the then proprietor, and some of his staff in the doorway. Other hotels in High Street at this time were the Victoria at number 52, the Half Moon at number 54, and the Waverley at number 78. The entrance to the Crown led to a flight of stairs to the bar and the residents' lounge, and another stairway opening into the dining room and a large ballroom – a favourite venue for dances and whist drives. The hotel closed in the late 1980s, reopening as the Crown Business Centre in 1993. To the right, Ayrshire-born Mrs Margaret Campbell peeks out of her husband William's boot and shoe shop, while next to this is Crown Close, which the *Hawick Advertiser* printworks shared with the premises of blacksmith William Telfer and his three employees.

Mrs Janet Lamb, photographed in the doorway of her baby linen and fancy goods shop at 59 High Street around 1908. She had started the business, living in the house above, a year or two before, on returning from Perth, Australia, with her husband, John, a joiner. This photograph appeared on a postcard, sent to Miss Marion Walker at Redfordgreen Farm, Roberton, on 9 August 1909, which carried the message: 'Do not think I dare take the road tomorrow it is so hot, nearly roasted on Sunday on yon bad road. Was pleased to see your mother has taken a holiday – hope it will do her good. Come down soon. J. Lamb.' Janet retired shortly after John's death in 1928 and sold the business to a Miss Rutherford, who was succeeded by H. M. Stormont. On his retiral in the late 1950s, the property was incorporated into the premises of Gaylor the optician. Janet died on 2 January 1941 and was buried in her husband's lair at Wellogate Cemetery.

HAWICK

The High Street in the summer of 1956. By this time the spread of chain stores, such as Woolworth's and Burton the tailor, was changing shopping habits as well as the character of town centres. The biggest impact on high streets, however, was made by the motor car. In 1920, when Hawick's High Street was busy with perhaps half a dozen horses and carts, Britain had only 591,000 licensed motor vehicles on the roads; by the time of this photograph there were 6.3 million and 30.5 million by 2003.

A 1903 photograph of the east end of High Street (the 'Coffin End') with the Central Hotel dividing North Bridge Street to the left and Bourtree Place to the right. The hotel was run by George Luff, 'a smart active little man' who had come to Hawick in the late 1870s from his native Brighton, by way of the Continent, in his profession as a waiter. Initially employed in the Tower Hotel, he went on to make his – sometimes unfavourable – impression on the town. He served the Wilton ward on the town council for three years and St James's Masonic Lodge as secretary for eighteen months. Typical of his gusto was the advertisement he placed in the *Hawick News* in February 1888: 'Masonic Lodge 424 will be expected to turn out well on Tuesday first. The fearless, energetic secretary, Bro. Luff will be present.' The streetlight fronting the premises was known as 'Luff's Lamp'. When the hotel closed in the spring of 1919 the building was bought for £2,300 by the Prudential Insurance Company and opened as their district office on 5 February 1920. They would occupy it until the mid-1950s. The ground floor of the building is now the Coffin End Restaurant, while the upper floors have had many tenants since the days of the Prudential.

High Street on a wet and cheerless afternoon around 1911. On the left, at number 61, is the boot- and shoemaker Stead & Simpson, while opposite is the grocer, Borthwick Turnbull. Next door to Turnbull's is Mrs Wilson's china shop on the O'Connell Street corner; the Glencairn Bar is on the opposite corner. Going down from the bar are Rule's newsagent's, Kyle the dairyman, Mrs Roy's toy shop, and Davidson Brothers' fishmonger's.

Photographed from the 'Coffin End' in the days before the Horse monument, the morning mist is clearing to reveal High Street busy with carters making their deliveries. On the Brougham Street corner is the Liberal Club (later Hawick Sports and Social Club), built for local members of the Liberal Party at a cost of £6,400 in 1894. The foundation stone was laid on 6 October that year by Mr John T. Laing of Linden Park.

An Albion Viking 26-seater omnibus coming onto High Street sometime in the late 1930s (by this time the 'Horse' was in place!). Built in 1930, the vehicle was used on local services by the bus company Adam Graham of High Street, who, along with many other operators across Scotland, was taken over by the SMT in 1935. A generation earlier, a John Graham was hiring out cabs from premises in Drumlanrig Square.

High Street, photographed on an afternoon in the late 1930s from the Brougham Street corner and showing Ralph Dodds & Sons' Green Café restaurant (now the Sugar Mountain sweet shop). Further down are the twin turrets of the Palace Theatre.

High Street on a wet afternoon in the early 1950s. On the left is the 1,100-seat Pavilion Theatre cinema, then owned by Scott's Theatres of Motherwell. It had a 30-feet-high screen and seat prices ranged from 9d. to 2s.3d. The programme started daily at 6.00 p.m. and changed twice weekly. Showing that week were the 1949 film *White Heat*, starring James Cagney as a 'mamma obsessed psychopath', and the North-West Frontier spectacular, *Gunga Din*, with Cary Grant, Douglas Fairbanks Jnr and Joan Fontaine. Hawick's other cinemas at that time were the Odeon at the Tower Knowe and The Theatre in Croft Road.

The premises of R.M. Virtue, the confectioner and fruit and vegetable merchant at 46 High Street, in the grip of the blaze that destroyed the building in October 1908. For a time during the incident, the premises of William Ross the chemist (on the near side) and Lauchlan Gentles the draper (on the other side) were also under threat. However the fire brigade arrived in time to save them, no doubt to cheers from the gathered crowd.

The inspection of the burnt-out shell of Virtue's shop the following morning.

Photographed in 1919, Provost George Heron Wilson CBE, flanked by the town's magistrates, councillors, and the Halbardier standing behind him, makes the proclamation that world war hostilities have ended. A detachment of the King's Own Scottish Borderers form the cordon, while the local Boy Scouts are lined up in Cross Wynd. As with communities across the country, Boy Scout troops were formed in Hawick and across Roxburghshire long before registration was centralised. The 1st Hawick Troop (5th Roxburgh) was registered with Imperial Headquarters, London, on 21 January 1925, when Scoutmaster Charles Dixon Oliver of Wellogate Villa had 32 Scouts and ten Rover Scouts. The 2nd Hawick Troop was registered on 12 February the same year, with 24 boys under Norman J. Sutherland of Gibson's Temperance Hotel and his assistant scout masters, James Lockhart of Victoria Road and Alec Waldie of Teviot Crescent.

An 'Exhibition of Fashions' was staged in the town hall in October 1906 by John W. Innes, the draper, milliner and costumier of 72 Botchergate, Carlisle. In the early twentieth century such exhibitions were staged in spring and autumn by local traders, but for a retailer to have travelled from as far as Carlisle was unusual in those days. The man seated to the front may be the 26-year-old Innes himself. His business is listed in the 1905 Carlisle trade directory as being at 56 Cliff Terrace, and from 1906 to 1910 in Botchergate, before vanishing.

Robert Nelson the shoemaker outside his shop at 6 O'Connell Street (now the car park) in the winter of 1907/08. Fellow traders in O'Connell Street at that time were Miller, the gasfitter, plumber and slater; Robert Elliot, another shoemaker; Jardine the grocer; Burns the butcher, whose family also kept a dairy; Cleghorn's laundry; and three fish restaurants – Mackie's, Maxwell's and Smith's. Originally from Middlebie in Dumfriesshire, Nelson lived with his wife Margaret (née Johnstone) and their daughter, Marion, at 15 Lothian Road. Aged 55 years, Margaret died in October 1908 at their later home, 5 Garfield Street. Robert died in May 1912, aged 56.

The tweed manufacturing Weensland Mill around 1907, when it was owned by Sime, Williamson & Co. It is overlooked from the right by Heronhill, the home of the manufacturer Robert Noble, and from the wooded hill behind by Thornwood, home of the auctioneer James Oliver (this is now the Mansefield House Hotel). Part of Weensland Mill was used as a barracks during the First World War. Most of the mill is now occupied by the Tregus Function Suite.

The 1892-built Hawick Post Office, on the corner of Croft Street and Bridge Street, photographed after the second storey was added to the right-hand end in 1904. The post office had been at 27 High Street since 1880, but by 1901, with an ever increasing volume of mail, it was deemed inadequate. The new building was designed by James P. Alison and the cost of £2,402 was paid for by James Oliver of Thornwood. In 1972 the sorting office moved to St George's Lane and this building was sold in 1993, becoming the appropriately named Stamper's pub.

From its introduction at Coventry Post Office in 1880, the use of the bicycle for deliveries soon spread across the country. Of this group of Hawick posties from the 1920s, only William John Elliot, in the centre, can be named.

Coming to Hawick after the First World War, John Hogg McGlynn ('Jock'), pictured here in his twenties, worked with the local post office until his retiral in the late 1940s.

Two horsedrawn carts – the horses in their decorative 'janglers' – pictured outside numbers 43 to 45 North Bridge Street in the early twentieth century. On the left are the premises of the dressmakers Hathorn and Wither, with the home of architect James P. Alison, who had designed the building, above. Born in 1863 at Dalkeith, where his father, Thomas, was a magistrate, James Alison came to Hawick in the 1880s. To the right, with the sign over the window, is the studio and home of John Edward Dodd Murray the photographer, who may have taken the photograph. Born in 1858, Murray opened his first photographic studio in the late 1880s on a site later taken by the post office. He moved to these new premises in November 1902, styling himself as an 'Artist, Photographer and Picture Framer'. Despite competition from Robert Bell and Thomas T. Wilkinson in High Street, Jenner & Co. in Exchange Arcade and G.A. Robinson, also in Bridge Street, 'Jed' (as Murray was popularly known) was 'Hawick's Photographer' and received business from the bicycle club, the operatic society, and each year's Cornet. He was Cornet himself in 1890 (his horse was called Oakwood Daisy).

With the milkman looking more like a charioteer, this early-twentieth-century milk delivery cart was photographed at the rear of the Teviotdale Dairy Company's premises in North Bridge Street. The business later became the Honeyburn & Teviotdale Dairy Co. Ltd, eventually owned by the Buttercup Dairy Co. of Easter Road, Leith. The milk bottle, introduced by the Express Dairy Company of London in the 1880s, was on its way by the time of this photograph, but it is not known when it came to Hawick.

This photograph of 1908, taken from the railway bridge, shows the North Bridge (built in 1832 by John and Thomas Smith), flanked on the left by the Carnegie Library at the foot of North Bridge Street, and Station Buildings on the right. Opened in 1904, Hawick Carnegie Library – built at cost of £10,000 – was one of 660 libraries in Britain financed by the Scots-born American industrialist and philanthropist, Andrew Carnegie (1835–1918). The clock belongs to Dickson's & Laing's Wilton Mills.

A flock of sheep passes into Duke Street on their way to market. They are driven by David Henderson of Cowlady Cottages and his dog Queenie, with Jake Scott, on the left, who farmed Branxholm Park Farm on the Carlisle road.

Andrew Oliver's auction market, photographed from the railway embankment in the early 1900s. Founded in 1817, it is claimed to have been the first auction market in Britain. From the left, across the top of the picture, Earl Street comes to the Trinity Street junction. Born the second son of James Oliver of Marlefield, Hope Farm, Eckford, in September 1793, Andrew Oliver was apprenticed to a solicitor in Kelso before starting on his own as a writer (a solicitor) in Annan. He came to Hawick in 1817 as a writer and auctioneer. Initially, the monthly sales were held in Slitrig Crescent, then Bourtree Place, and it was not until 1883 that his firm bought this site and business expanded. It closed in 1992 and within the year the site was taken by a supermarket.

The Trinity Bar, on the corner of Duke Street and Noble Place, photographed around 1904 when William McGill was the licence holder. It was built in the 1890s and by the 1930s it was run by Thomas Mack, and although others, including Russell Crosbie (brother of 1950s Cornet, Thomas E. Crosbie), have passed through, it is still known as Mack's Bar. The cellar windows at pavement level are long gone and around 1990 the whole premises were revamped.

John Robertson's grocer's and provision merchant's shop on the corner of Earl Street and Trinity Street, c.1908. Of the 38 grocers then in Hawick, Robertson, as president of the Total Abstinence Society, was not one of the eighteen licensed to sell liquor! Although now a dwelling, many recall it as Lizzie Fordyce's corner shop.

A horse and cart makes its way along the flooded Teviot Crescent, possibly in the winter of 1928/29. As regular as these inundations have been over the years, the 'Hawick Flood' of August 1767 was the worst, earning a mention in the first *Statistical Account* of the 1790s. Following a cloud burst over the source of the Slitrig, on that occasion the river rose 23 feet in two hours. In Hawick, the parochial school, a corn mill, and an entire street of fifteen houses, with two of the inhabitants, were carried away by the waters.

Glendinning's (later Nichol's) Garage in Teviot Crescent, photographed in the 1920s on a day when a Ford Model T belonging to Mr Palmer Douglas of Denholm was in for a service. Standing in the centre of the group of men is the threshing mill contractor John Thomson (1898–1980), whose parents, William and Jane Thomson, appear with his sister Elizabeth in the photograph of Adderstonshiels Cottages on page 84.

The 2/4 Royal Scots Fusiliers on Slitrig Crescent during their march from the town's railway station to Stobs Camp. Formed at Kilmarnock, Ayrshire, in October 1914, they served in the British Isles throughout the war and were disbanded in Ireland in May 1918.

Dovemount Place from the corner of Commercial Road to Wilton Place, with the railway station on the right. On the left, rounding from Commercial Road and running to Laing Terrace, is Station Buildings with the premises of Allan Watt & Sons, newsagents, stationers, booksellers and printers (they used this photograph on one of the postcards they printed in the basement). From around 1888, they were also Dovemount Place Post Office. Next door, under the pestle and mortar, is the chemist W.J. Kearney. Although no Kodak signs are evident in the window, he billed himself in the town's 1906 directory as a 'Dispensing Photo Chemist', offering, 'All the popular Papers, Plates and films – Developing and Toning Solutions', and, although plate and film developing was a speciality, there was also a dark room available for amateurs. Next is J. Bowie, dyers and French cleaners, and on the Laing Terrace junction is a shop later occupied by McDonald's restaurant (abeit not of the famous chain!). The run of buildings beyond starts with the Station Hotel, managed by James Wilson at the time of this photograph, and continues with Anderson the confectioner and tobacconist, Lindsay the fishmonger, Miss McMahon the dressmaker, and Wilson's Temperance Hotel.

Robert McDonald the restaurateur, and his staff, outside his premises at 5 Dovemount Place (now the Shugonda Balti House) on the corner of Laing Terrace in the 1920s. Offering breakfasts, dinners and teas, the business was well situated to attract rail travellers.

Gifted by James Glenny, Charles John Wilson and George Murray Wilson of the tweed manufacturers, Messrs Wilson & Glenny of Langlands and Ladylaw Mills, the £2,000 Swimming Baths on Bath Street (they also gifted the site) were opened on Saturday, 24 May 1913. From the platform at the opening ceremony, Charles Wilson said he had formed the idea following a health visit to the Salt Brine Baths at Droitwich some twelve years earlier and had consulted Droitwich on the design. Measuring 75 feet by 30 feet, the pool ranged in depth from 3½ to 6½ feet, and was at that time one of the best in the country. After the opening ceremony, Hawick Amateur Swimming Club – who were now able to abandon the river – gave diving exhibitions and Mr John Boyle, swimming instructor for Leith School Board, assisted by Misses Bella and Annie Wood, 'gave an interesting display of scientific and ornamental swimming'. The pool served the town until the opening of the Teviot Leisure Centre, on the site of the railway station, in July 1982.

Flanked by Duke Street on the left and the railway station above Mansfield Road opposite, the river's summer trickle passes under the 42-feet-high Teviot Viaduct down to the North Bridge in the summer of 1915. Demolition work on the viaduct began on 1 September 1975.

The railway station, photographed around 1903 from an upper window of the Station Hotel in Dovemount Place. At the time, 'The first class family and commercial hotel offered home comforts at moderate charges' and, as an extra service, an 'Electric Bell rings in Hotel Five Minutes before the Train arrives in the Station'. This view shows, from the left, the goods yard, signal box, water tower and the station building, beyond which was the main line. Today's view from the window shows the Teviotdale Leisure Centre. The first service train from Edinburgh arrived at Hawick on 1 November 1849 (it was run by the North British Railway), but not until July 1862 was the Waverley Route completed to Carlisle and beyond. In latter days, Hawick was one hour and thirty-three minutes from Edinburgh and eight hours and forty-eight minutes from London's Kings Cross. The last passenger train passed through for London on the night of Sunday, 5 January 1969; the last goods train ran the following April, and work on lifting the track commenced on 18 April 1971.

The signal box at the station was built in 1873 and controlled railway traffic between Hawick and Stobs Station, four miles to the south, as well as traffic within the station area, at the sheds and sidings, and coal trains to the gasworks. It was demolished on 13 July 1972.

A party of men departing from Hawick Railway Station, to a rousing send off, in the early 1920s. They were important enough to warrant pipers, drummers, a Boy Scout – and another photographer (upper right) – but who were they?

The D20 class 4-4-0 railway engine, No. 62387, with a train on the southbound line out of Hawick Railway Station in the 1930s. Then based at Heaton railway sheds in Newcastle-upon-Tyne, she was one of over fifty locomotives of this model built at Darlington for the North Eastern Railway. She was scrapped by November 1957. In the background are the houses of Wilton Hill Terrace.

St Mary's Church from Kirkstile. According to the ancient *Chronicle of Melrose*, a church has occupied this site overlooking the town since 1214, when the original St Mary's was erected. In his report for the 1830s *New Statistical Account*, the Rev. J.A. Wallace gave his opinion that not only was this 1764 building 'devoid of every architectural embellishment', but with only 704 sittings was 'inadequate for a parish population of 5,998'. It was the parish church until the new church in Buccleuch Street was built in 1844. Despite efforts to erase it from the photograph, Welsh the cycle agent's advertisement on the wall to the right of the stairway can just be made out.

John Hillerton outside his grocer shop at 21 Howegate around 1925/26, flanked by his nephew Bill Chalmers (to the right) and Bill's pal, Frank McQuade. Born at Bedrule, John came to Hawick in 1919 after his demob from the Royal Military Police and served the local constabulary until 1921, when he married his wife Annie. They took over the premises and the house above from William Bainbridge who had marketed the premises as a 'First Class Restaurant – serving Dinners, Teas, Fish Suppers, confectionery, Ice cream, Aerated Waters and all the Latest Waters'. John returned to the police as a reservist during the Second World War, but while attending a major fire in Autumn 1944 was so thoroughly soaked that he succumbed to pneumonia and died on 24 October.

Although much was written in word and song about the Auld Mid Raw following its demolition in 1884, little apart from census returns has survived of its earlier history. When it was built, and by whom, remains a mystery. For decades before demolition it was unfit for habitation, but the town council were powerless to condemn it. It was left to those who could spare the cost to buy the houses, one by one, and hand them over to the council who, with the last purchase, brought the whole edifice down. The 1861 census return shows the eleven houses in the row were home to 171 people – an average density of 15.5 per house. In the 2001 census return, Hawick's average household density was 2.13 and for Scotland as a whole, 2.27.

Oh! had thae rugged stanes a tongue,
What sermons they could preach;
What tales the mouldering rafters tell
Had they the power o' speech.
When news o' Flodden's day o' dool
Made dark baith hut and ha',
And hapless widows mourned the brave
In the auld Mid Raw.

Anon.

As can be seen from this 1906 view, taken from roughly the same spot as the previous photograph, the demolition of Auld Mid Raw revealed the spaciousness of Drumlanrig Square and gave a clear sight from the West Gate at the end of the Loan to the Howegate.

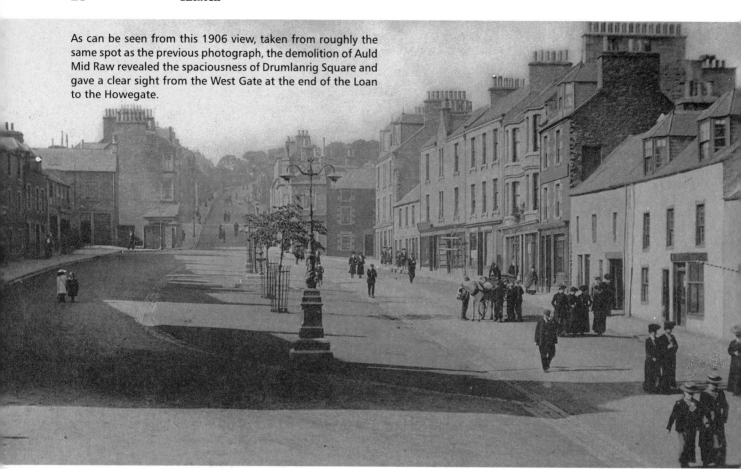

Drumlanrig Square, photographed around 1911 from the Loan end. By this time the square had been graced with the Brown Memorial Fountain and clock. When 72-year-old auctioneer and house factor William Brown died at his home, Salisbury House, in Forth Street, Alloa, on 20 September 1908, his bequest for the building of the memorial showed he had not forgotten his Border roots, nor the Hawick he had left in his teens. Built to a design by local architect James P. Alison, FRIBA, the stone was fashioned by Alexander Mackay and David Morran, stone masons of Holland Street, Aberdeen, and constructed by local builders Marshall & Company.

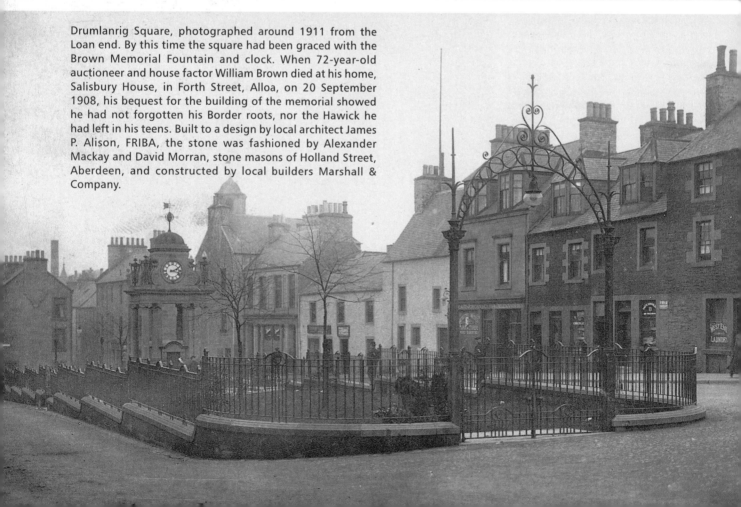

The governor and staff of the Hawick Combination Poorhouse (or workhouse), photographed around 1905. Entered at the junction of Drumlanrig Square and the Loan, it was built in 1857 at a cost of £4,000 and could accommodate 133 inmates. It served not only Hawick, but also the surrounding parishes, from Canonbie to Lilliesleaf. The 1881 census records the eldest resident as 84-year-old Ann Kennedy, a domestic servant, and the youngest as two-month-old Janet Scott. During the First World War it was used as an army hospital and in the 1930s was renamed Drumlanrig Poor Law Institution, serving only Roxburghshire. With improving social conditions, it later became a geriatric hospital, a use which continued until 1994. The building is now derelict.

Designed by the Edinburgh architect Reginald Fairlie (1883–1952), the Dominican Nuns' St Margaret's Home for Incurables, in the convent grounds in Myreslawgreen, was opened on Monday, 24 September 1934, by the Archbishop of Edinburgh and St Andrews, the Most Reverend Andrew Thomas Joseph McDonald (1871–1950). Also at the ceremony were the Earl and Countess of Minto, Major General Sir Walter Maxwell-Scott of Abbotsford, and Lady Maxwell-Scott who gifted the statue of St Margaret, the work of Thomas J. Burns of Messrs Donaldson & Burns of Edinburgh, in the niche above the entry. Nuns of the Third Order of St Dominic had come to Hawick around 1909, taking a house in Buccleuch Street before their convent in Myreslawgreen was completed in 1913. This convent closed in the late 1990s when the last two nuns, Sister Asumpta and Sister Margaret, retired to St Joseph's Retreat in Sussex. It is now occupied by district council offices.

The Moat, Mote or Motte in the field beyond Drumlanrig Primary School, photographed around 1912, when an archaeological examination found it to be ringed with a flat-bottomed ditch ranging in width from 28 feet to 14 feet and in depth from 7 feet to 4 feet. Described as a grass-covered truncated cone, its 41-feet diameter top is flat and stands 25 feet above a 97-feet diameter base. The examination included an exploratory dig into the ditch, where a bone needle and a coin of Henry II of England (1133–89), now on display at the Wilton Lodge Museum, were found. Victorian theories of it having been a Druid temple or burial site have now been dispelled and it is recognised as a twelfth-century castle site, possibly built by the Lovel family who controlled Hawick at that time.

Buccleuch Street from Sandbed around 1914. The first premises on the left (1 Sandbed) belonged to the watchmaker, jeweller, silversmith and optician – and magistrate and justice of the peace – Alexander Sutherland Lawson. A native of Hawick, he appears to have started the business in May 1864, as a 20-year-old, and lived for a time, with his wife Catherine, at 6 Beaconsfield Terrace. He also sold cups, medals and Masonic jewels, 'at lowest possible prices', and through his shipping agency business handled tickets 'to all parts of the world by the Best Lines of Steamers and Sailing Ships'. When he died in October 1916, he and Catherine were living above the shop. Next, with the young man standing in the doorway, is W. & J. Kennedy the bookseller, and, into Buccleuch Street, Peter Scott's knitwear factory. Founded in 1878 for the manufacture of woollen underwear, 'Pesco' moved from the Tabernacle in Kirkwynd to this new factory around 1904. Over the years they have shifted from 'underwear' to 'outerwear' and today lead the field in exporting top of the range cashmere and wool knitwear. On the opposite corner, 2 Buccleuch Street (restored in 1992), is the grocer and provision dealer James O. Elliot, the eponymous founder of which compiled the first history of Hawick in 1825. Under the sunshade next door are the premises of the cabinetmakers and upholsterers, W. Scott & Sons.

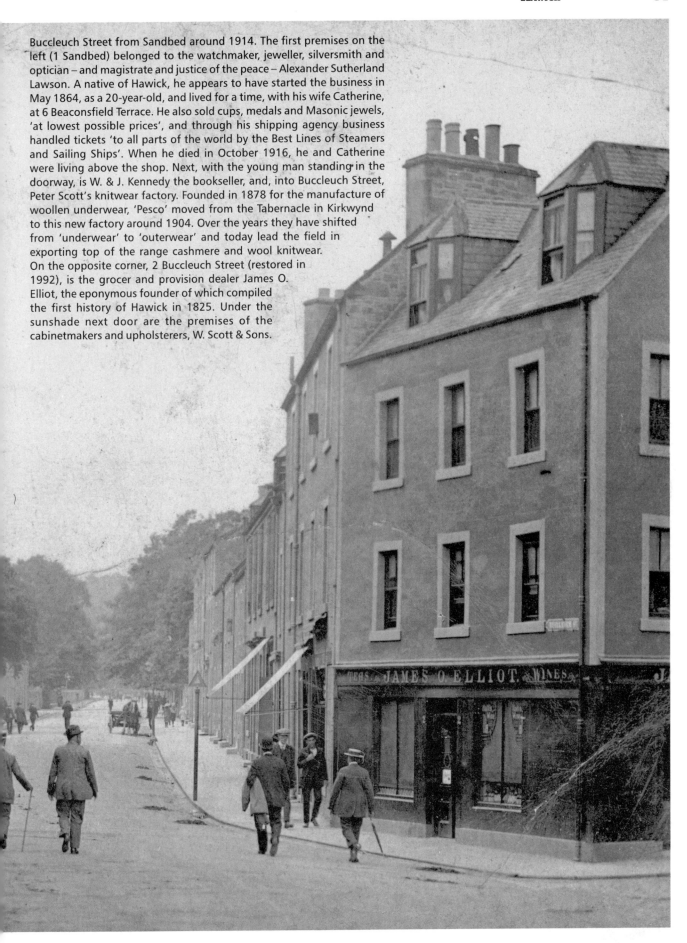

The interior of W. & J. Kennedy's bookshop on Sandbed. They were also, as can be seen from the table display, stationers and picture dealers. The proprietors were brothers: John W. Kennedy, shown in the 1881 census return as a 25-year-old bachelor and bookseller, living above the premises with his 63-year-old widowed mother, Christian Kennedy; and Walter Phillips Kennedy, also 25-years-old in 1881 and a science teacher and bookseller living at 8 Beaconsfield Terrace with his wife, Jane. The business disappeared in the 1960s, but the name lives on – a copy of J. Hicks's *Wanderings by the Lochs and Streams of Assynt* (1855), bearing the ticket 'W. & J. Kennedy of Hawick' appeared at auction in 2004.

A similar view of Sandbed as the one on the previous pages, but dating from the early 1950s. By this time Lawson the watchmaker had been taken over by A.J. Aitken the tobacconist, but Kennedy the bookseller was still in business. On the right, Elliot the grocer had become Burns the ironmonger. Into Orrock Place – named after Alexander Orrock (1652–1711) who was appointed minister to Hawick on 17 October 1694 – is the Ewe and Lamb public house.

Lawson Bridge, linking St George's Lane with the Common Haugh, photographed shortly after its opening in 1904. Across the river stands Elliot, McTaggart & Co.'s skinworks and to the right, Ellabank, the manse of St George's Church. The gentleman on the left may be Bailie Alex S. Lawson (1842–1916), the watchmaker and jeweller of 1 Sandbed, who gifted the bridge to the town. A native of Hawick, he served as a town councillor and magistrate for 43 years and was president of the Callants' Club in 1913. The bridge was demolished and replaced in the summer of 1988.

Built in 1865, on land gifted by the Duke of Buccleuch, this new school replaced the two-room 1826 school in Orrock Place. It was initially named Buccleuch Elementary School, but was informally known as 'Dodds' Schule' after its rector, Anthony Dodds (1819–1887). Four years after this photograph was taken in 1904, the school underwent a £10,000 rebuild by the architect Joseph Blaike of Park Street, Hawick, and opened as Buccleuch Higher Grade School on 22 August 1908. Around the 61 feet by 34 feet 6 inches central hall, the ground floor had thirteen double-desk classrooms to accommodate over 600 pupils, while the first floor had six higher-grade classrooms for 220 children. There were also two art rooms, a physics laboratory, a chemical laboratory, a manual instruction block and a cookery and laundry block. With the new building came a new rector, Mr W.L. Thompson, formerly of Allan Glen's School, Glasgow. In 1915 it was renamed Hawick High School. The building was lost to an extensive fire in the early morning of 23 December 1925, but, as will be seen from the photograph on the next page, the Phoenix did arise and the rebuilt school opened in October 1928.

The greens of the Buccleuch and Hawick bowling clubs, the new Hawick High School, and, to the right, the bell tower of the old parish church, photographed in the summer of 1929. Instituted in 1854, Hawick Bowling Club may be the oldest in the Borders and held the region's first open tournament in 1872. Equally active, with a membership of over 100, is its neighbour – and at times rival – the Buccleuch Bowling Club, founded in 1872. To the right is Hawick Parish Church, built in 1844 to cater for an expanding town and congregation. On opening it took the title 'Parish' from St Mary's. In the late 1980s the church building succumbed to dry rot and a final service was held in January 1989. Its site was taken by Frank Scott Court, a nineteen-flat sheltered housing complex opened in July 2002 and named to commemorate an ex-provost, Frank Scott, who died in March 2001.

Buccleuch Bowling Club members and friends outside their pavilion, possibly at the end of the 1904/05 season, with that year's president, Robert Beattie, in front of the right-hand pillar. The trophy cannot be identified as it is no longer held by the club.

The Cottage Hospital, on the banking above the Carlisle road, photographed from the cricket ground. It dates from 1885, when it was built by public subscription. The left gable of the building has an inscribed foundation stone: 'This stone was laid with Masonic Honours on the 30 August 1884 by the Rt. Hon., the Earl of Mar and Kellie. The Most Worshipful, The Grand Master Mason of Scotland'. One year and a day later, the twelve-bed hospital was opened by the Duchess of Buccleuch. On his visit to the town on 3 December 1924, the Prince of Wales laid the foundation stone of the Esmund Elliot Memorial Ward, a new addition to the complex which was financed (£2,250) by the Elliots of Minto to commemorate the life of their son, a lieutenant in the Scots Guards who was killed in action on 6 August 1918. Under current planning, the hospital is due to be replaced soon.

In 1935 the Cottage Hospital's Silver Jubilee was marked by celebrations in the form of fund-raising events, involving voluntary organisations, the churches, athletic and football clubs, and the fire brigade. Festooned with flags – and a pair of trousers – Hawick's first motorised fire engine no doubt added colour to the parade. Topped by a 35-feet escape ladder, the Merryweather engine was equipped with a three-cylinder Hatfield reciprocating water pump, driven off the engine through a clutch and drive shaft to deliver 450 to 500 gallons of water per minute. It came to Hawick in August 1918, but the registration number LP9739, issued in London between September 1915 and July 1916, indicates that it was around two years old and was probably bought second hand.

As part of the Hospital's Silver Jubilee parade, Thomson's lorry carries the 'Missionary's Nightmare' through Drumlanrig Square.

Also thought to have taken part in the parade is this float, photographed in Volunteer Park, with the seven 'Heavenly Virtues' ready to join the firemen and the 'Missionary's Nightmare'. Third from the left is Nan Elder, who later married Bill Walsh, a master joiner, and moved to the Johnstone area of Renfrewshire.

The putting green in Wilton Lodge Park in the 1920s, with Wilton Lodge breaking the line of trees in the background (the green is now the site of the crazy golf course). If tradition is to be believed, the original fortified house, possibly a peel tower (a round fortified house), was erected by the Langlands, or Longueville, family in the late thirteenth century and remained in their hands until 1783 when Robert Langlands sold the estate and moved to Edinburgh. The estate then passed through a number of hands, one of whom, Lord Napier of Ettrick and Thirlestane, changed the name to Wilton Lodge. The town council purchased the house and its 107-acre estate in 1890 and, after serving as Wilton Lodge Academy and a period of dormancy, it opened as Hawick Museum and Park in October 1910.

Edward, Prince of Wales, and the civic party at the war memorial in Wilton Lodge Park, during his whistle-stop visit to Hawick on Monday 3 December 1924. Having spent the previous night at Minto House, he was gone by eleven o'clock that morning. The day started on the balcony of the town hall, where he acknowledged the cheering crowds – schools and shops had closed for the morning – before going on to the Cottage Hospital to lay the foundation stone of the Esmond Elliot Memorial Ward, and to the war memorial by way of Spetchman's Haugh, where he opened the newly built Laurie Bridge. After laying a wreath at the memorial, he joined the civic dignitaries for this photograph. *Front row* (left to right): the Right Honourable, the 5th Earl of Minto (Victor Lariston Garnet Elliot-Murray-Kynynmound); the Countess of Minto; John R. Purdom (Town Clerk); His Royal Highness, the Prince of Wales; James Renwick, provost from 1922 to 1928; Mrs Renwick; His Grace, the 8th Duke of Buccleuch (Walter John Montagu-Douglas-Scott); and John Waldie, Burgh Officer. *Second row:* John Dick, Burgh Officer; Cllr Thomas B. Redpath; Bailie Francis Boles; Bailie Andrew Landles; Bailie George Brydon; Bailie George Gass, Burgh Treasurer; and Cllr James C. Bonsor. *Third row*: James Conn of Blinkbonny, Burgh Chamberlain; Cllr Robert Inglis; Cllr Adam Turnbull; Cllr David K. Roy; and Cllr William S. Nichol. *Fourth row*: Cllr James Hogg; Cllr Richard Laidlaw; Judge Stephen Anderson; Cllr David Fisher; and Charles B. McCall, Depute Town Clerk. Featuring a bronze statue mounted on a six-feet pedestal – 'Spirit of Youth Triumphing over Evil' by the sculptor Alexander J. Leslie – the towering 27-feet Doddington-stone cenotaph was designed by James B. Dunn ARSA of Edinburgh (1861–1930) and constructed by Messrs J. Marshall of Hawick. It was unveiled in October 1921 by the Right Honourable Robert Munro, Secretary of State for Scotland (1916–1922).

Spanning the River Teviot, the Laurie Bridge links the 'Lido' at Spetchman's Haugh with Wilton Lodge Park. A native of Hawick, Walter Laurie (1858–1923) had spent his life in the liquor trade, appearing in the 1881 census as a barman lodging with George Montgomery at 7 Back Row. At the time of his death he was living at 23 Bridge Street and running a successful wine and spirit business from premises at 13 Teviot Crescent. His bequest of £1,350 built this bridge, opened by the Prince of Wales during his visit to Hawick on 3 December 1924.

A woman and a boy, possibly mother and son, on the grass fronting Wilton Lodge in the summer of 1927. The fountain in the background is inscribed with the following: 'This fountain was bequeathed to the Burgh by Gilbert Davidson Esq., Banker in Hawick'. Agent for the British Linen Bank in High Street – in 1797 this became the first bank to establish a branch in Hawick – Davidson appears in the 1881 census return as an unmarried 47-year-old banker and farmer living at Kirkton. He employed eight men, but the record fails to show whether they were tellers or farm hands! He died at Taudlaw on 21 March 1896, leaving the bulk of his estate to a nephew, William Davidson Adam, then a clerk with the Town & County Bank at Aberdeen.

The elderly gentlemen of the Langlands Club, recalling the family that occupied Wilton Lodge from the late thirteenth century until 1783, who read their newspapers, played their dominoes, and reminisced in a room in the house. This photograph dates from the early 1900s.

Two little girls flanked by the Patriotic Monument and the bandstand in Wilton Lodge Park and photographed around 1918. The bandstand, erected in the late 1890s, was probably from Walter McFarlane's Saracen Head Foundry in Glasgow. The Patriotic Memorial, raised in memory of the 23 officers and men of Hawick and district who died in the Boer War (1899–1902), was unveiled by Field Marshall The Earl Roberts, then commander-in-chief of the British Army, at a ceremony on Saturday, 22 August 1903. The 22-feet-high monument features an eight-feet-high bronze-cast soldier, the work of the sculptor William Birnie Rhind ARSA (1853–1933). This sits atop a square pedestal of Northumberland freestone, each face carrying an inscribed bronze panel. The front panel, surmounted by the badge of the KOSB, in part bears the message: 'You do well to keep their memories green', a quotation from a speech made by Joseph Chamberlain, the Colonial Secretary, at Grahamstown in South Africa in February 1903. The other panels bear, respectively, the names of the officers and men killed in action, and those who died of their wounds later.

Field Marshal The Earl Roberts and his 20-carriage retinue on their way from a civic luncheon in the council chamber of the town hall to unveil the Patriotic Memorial in Wilton Lodge Park, on the afternoon of Saturday, 22 August 1903. Possibly under the influence of Lord Minto, who had served with the field marshal in the Second Afghan War of 1878–80, this was Lord Roberts's second visit to Hawick that year. From the previous evening, his two-day itinerary included the civic reception, a visit to Stobs Camp and the unveiling.

A 1908 photograph of John Forbes's Buccleuch, later 'Royal', Nursery. A native of Logierait, south of Pitlochry, Perthshire, John Forbes came to Hawick in the late 1880s with his Dunfermline-born wife, Margaret, from Killiechassie House, by Aberfeldy. He had been a gardener there and came to work at Wilton Lodge. In 1870 he started a small nursery in north Hawick before moving to this larger site, where he employed four men and two boys. He served a three year term on Hawick Town Council and, in the 1880s, he and Margaret lived at the Brewery on Slitrig Road with their four children, Archibald, Jessie, Maggie and Isabella. In 1907 the business was granted the Royal Warrant and in 1908 became a limited company. In his specialist field of florists' flowers, he was responsible for improving the strains of *Pentstemons, Antirrhinums* and *Pansies*, and at his death in September 1909, in his 68th year, was considered Scotland's oldest and ablest nurseryman. Across the railway line, to the east, is Wellogate Cemetery where the first internment, on 13 July 1849, was of seventeen-year-old Robert Turnbull of Kirkwynd who had died of consumption.

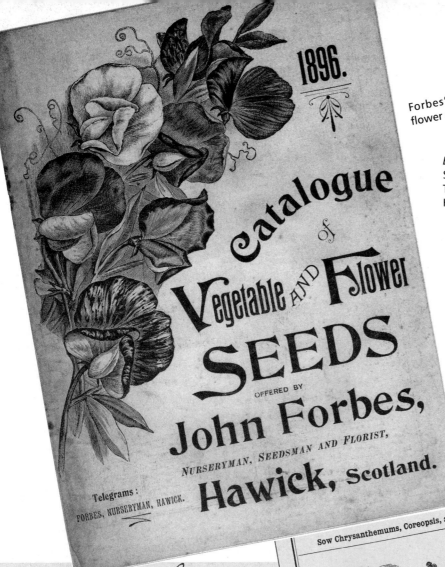

Forbes's annual vegetable and flower catalogue for 1896.

Bottom left: A Forbes invoice, dated 30 September 1898 and addressed to James Turnbull, grocer and spirit merchant at 51 High Street, Hawick.

A page from the floral section of Forbes's catalogue, featuring *Humulus japonicus*, 'a useful plant for verandahs', Hollyhocks, and the hardy annual *Linum grandiflorum*.

25

Sow Chrysanthemums, Coreopsis, and Corn Flower for cutting to fill vases, &c.

Humulus japonicus (Annual Hop).   *Hollyhock.*   *Linum grandiflorum rubrum.*

No.	NAME.	Hard. duratn.	Colour.	Hgt.in Feet.	Packet. s. d.	REMARKS.
						Free-blooming and hardy annuals, *G. tricolor* is sweet-scented
164	**Gilia** achillæfolia major	h a	blue	2	0 3	
165	tricolor	h a	various	1	0 3	Splendid bedding annuals, with large funnel-shaped flowers, suitable for any situation
166	**Godetia,** Bijou	h a	wh.rose spots	1½	0 3	
167	Lady Albemarle ...per oz., 1/6	h a	crimson	1½	0 3	
168	Duchess of Albany	h a	white	1	0 3	Valuable when young as a table plant
169	The Bride	h a	white & crim.	1	0 3	Showy and hardy border annuals
170	Whitneyi	h a	blush & crim.	1	0 3	Very effective varieties of the Sunflower ; *H. cucumerifolius* (the *miniature* variety), is valuable for cutting for vases, &c.
171	**Grevillea** robusta	g s	or. foliage	4	0 6	
172	**Hawkweed,** *mixed*	h a	various	1	0 3	
173	**Helianthus** argophyllus	h a	yellow	4	0 3	
174	cucumerifolius	h a	yellow	4	0 3	
175	globosus fistulosus	h h a	gold & yel.	3	0 3	Showy and effective Everlastings, suitable for church and house decoration
176	**Helichrysum** bracteatum	h h a	yellow	2	0 3	
177	album	h h a	white	1½	0 3	Sweet-scented bedding or pot plant
178	monstrosum,double,*finest mixed*	h h p	various	1½	1/-, 2/6	Singular and showy annual
179	**Heliotropium,** *finest mixed*	h a	wh. & brown	6	0 6	Saved from fine double flowers ; showy for borders
180	**Hibiscus** Africanus major	h p	various	2	0 3	*Money Flower* ; showy for borders
181	**Hollyhock,** fine mixed, double	h p	pur. & white	4	cl.	Elegant for pots or mounds
182	**Honesty,** mixed	h h p	rose		cl.	Useful plants for verandahs, &c.
183	**Humea** elegans	h a	var. foliage	3	0 3	A valuable garnishing plant
184	**Humulus** japonicus (*Annual Hop*)	h a	frosted folge.	2	cl.	A charming pot plant
185	variegatus	g p	rosy scarlet.	2	0 3	Exquisite and well-known climbers
186	**Ice Plant**	h h a	various	1	0 3	Good border plants ; useful for cutting
187	**Impatiens** Sultani	h a	various		0 6	Pretty for edgings
188	**Ipomœa,** *choice mixed*	h a	bright blue.		0 3	
189	**Jacobæa,** double, dwarf, *mixed*	h a	various		1 0	Showy bedding annuals, thriving in any good garden soil
190	**Kaulfussia** amelloides	h a	various		0 6	
191	**Larkspur,** branching	h a	various		0 3	Showy climbers, useful for covering trellises, arbours, &c.
192	Dwarf Rocket, mixed, per oz.,6d.	h a	pink		0 3	
193	Hyacinth-flowered (*Everlasting Pea*)	h p	white	6	0 3	Pretty dwarf annuals, adapted for edgings or rockwork
194	**Lathyrus** latifolius	h a	blue		0 3	
195	albus	h a	various		0 3	Slightly fragrant ; good for bees
196	**Leptosiphon** densiflorus	h a	rose		0 3	Fine for beds and mixed borders
197	hybridus	h a	white & yel.		0 3	Very effective hardy annual
198	roseus	h a	various	1	2	Beautiful plant for the greenhouse
199	**Limnanthes** Douglasii...per oz., 6d.	h a	crimson	2	0 3	Very showy and useful for borders
200	**Linaria,** *mixed*	g b	purple		1 0	
201	**Linum** grandiflorum rubrum, oz., 6d.	g b	red		0 3	
202	**Lisianthus** Russellianus					
203	**Love-lies-bleeding**...per oz., 6d.					

Invoice (bottom left):

BUCCLEUCH NURSERIES,
HAWICK, SCOTLAND.   Sept 30   189

J. Turnbull Esq
Grocer
51 High St
Hawick

To John Forbes,
Nurseryman, Seedsman, Florist,
AND
New Plant Merchant.

To Goods as per Invoice   1 2 4
July 21 18 Bedding Begonias   - 6 -
Aug 10 6 Bush Soil   - 9 -
      11 4 "   "   "   - 6 -
      1 day of Gardener   5 - 4
                                                    £ 2 7 4

Settled per Contra
John Forbes
J. F.

A 1908 photograph of the Rustic Bridge in the grounds of Linden Park House, near Hornshole. The house and the bridge were designed by local architect John Guthrie for Walter Laing (1820–1895) of Dickson's & Laing's, the tweed and hosiery manufacturer on Commercial Road. The bridge spanned the Trow Burn which was dammed to operate a turbine-driven electricity generator which supplied the house.

Linnwood Mill, photographed around 1900. To the right is Linnwood House, at that time occupied by the solicitor John Oliver. The mill, powered by a lade off the Slitrig Water, opened in 1804 and was one of Hawick's earliest woollen mills. It had closed by 1905 and the site lay derelict until the early 1930s, when it was cleared for local authority housing.

The Town Crier, Alexander Stainton, or 'Alec the Bellman' as he was known, photographed at Miller's Knowes in the early 1920s. He held the position from 1905 until his death in December 1926, aged 73. A wool frame knitter, he lived at Wilton Crescent with his parents, Samuel and Sarah Stainton, until his thirties when he married Janet Riddell.

After an inaugural eight-mile cross-country run, Teviotdale Harriers Club was officially formed at a meeting in the Tower Hotel on Thursday, 24 January 1889. There was a membership of twelve 'gentlemen' who resolved 'to promote athletics, especially in the prosecution of cross-country running during winter months'. By the spring that year the membership had grown to 30 and, with ups and downs along the track since, the club is still running. It is Scotland's third oldest Harriers club in continuous existence, following Clydesdale Harriers (1885) and Maryhill Harriers (1888). This 1913 photograph shows some of the members wearing their maroon vests which had a distinctive 'THC' logo on the front (hidden by the competition numbers).

Hawick High School rugby team, photographed in Wilton Lodge Park sometime between 1917 and 1920.

Middle: The Hawick seven-a-side rugby team that won the 1927 Five Border Sports. *Front row* (left to right): J. Fraser; G.R. Cairns (captain); D. Patterson (president); Douglas S. Davies; and William B. Welsh (Scottish internationalist). *Back row*: W.A. McTaggart (Cornet of 1930 and later managing director of Pringle Scotland); A.C. Pinder; Andrew Bowie; and R.N.R. Storrie.

Hawick's Pleasant Sunday Afternoon rugby team c.1928–30, possibly photographed to show off their new gold-banded jerseys. Founded in 1875 by John Blackman, a 41-year-old Birmingham draper, the Pleasant Sunday Afternoon Organisation was, initially, an evangelical movement aimed at young men who found Sunday afternoon bible classes 'so blessed dull'. From an initial meeting of 120, the movement grew and, within a decade, spread out of Birmingham into the Black Country. There was also a 'Pleasant Monday Evening Meeting' for women. What made the P.S.A. different was the realisation that young men needed more than hymn singing and bible readings, and its ancillary agencies included labour bureaux, penny banks, saving clubs, sickness and burial societies, and football clubs. By the time it reached Hawick in 1919, it was a national organisation. The earliest, or earliest surviving, records of Hawick's P.S.A. are from 1931/32 when Tom Young was captain, but the founders were Messrs D. Paterson, D. Stavert and Bailie A.J. Hislop (club president 1920/21). In the 1927/28 season it won the semi-junior league while captained by T. Kyle. Regrettably, no records of the team in this photograph survive, nor have any of them been identified.

This photograph bore the caption: 'Hawick Orient Football Club, 1909/10', but research has failed to reveal details either of the club's origins or its demise. However, as there are fifteen team members, it is supposed that it was a rugby club and not, despite the apparent roundness of the ball, a soccer team. The word 'Orient' in the name may hold a clue – the London soccer club, Leyton Orient, is said to have taken the word from the Orient Shipping Company that employed one of its early players. Could there have been a sailor in this team?

Hawick Rugby Football Club's 1st Fifteen for the season 1912/13, when, of the 25 games played, they won seventeen, lost seven and drew one, gaining 226 points for, 96 against. *Front row*: T. Wilson; D. Shannon; G. Johnstone; and E.W. Anderson. *Middle row*: R. Edgar; G. Wilson; W.E. Kyle (captain and international player); Wattie R. Sutherland (internationalist); W. Burnett; G. Brown; and W.R. Tait. *Back row*: G.W.T. Laing; R.H.L. Watson; G. Johnstone; and A.P. Turnbull. (The men in suits cannot be named.)

The ladies chorus in Hawick Amateur Opera Company's 1936 25th anniversary production, *Rose Marie*, the last they would perform in the Pavilion Theatre on High Street. Under the baton of musical director, William Campbell, and the guidance of producer, Gordon Stamford, the *Hawick Advertiser* reported that '. . . nothing finer [had] been produced locally for a very long time'. Only two of the 30 'Totem Girls' can be named – Nanie Farries (front row, second from left) and Netta Wilson (back row, seventh from left). Founded in 1910, the company's first production, the Gilbert and Sullivan operetta, *HMS Pinafore*, was staged the following March in the Pavilion. Gilbert and Sullivan's works held sway until 1930 when it produced *The Country Girl*. Its most recent production (2004) was a staging of Rodgers and Hammerstein's *Carousel* under the direction of Jean Wintrope. She joined the company in 1948, playing the lead in *The Country Girl*.

Hawick Saxhorn Band was born of a petition presented to the magistrates, who called a public meeting on 29 October 1855 for the purpose of forming a town band. Money was forthcoming, £10 from the magistrates and a further £50 from a public subscription (and a little on the rates). Samuel Stainton, the parish church precentor (choir master), was elected leader (he died in October 1894). At this time, the valved brass instruments designed by the Belgian musician and inventor Antoine Joseph (Adolphe) Sax (1814–1894) were popular, hence, perhaps, the choice of his instruments. Of the 40 applicants, fourteen were chosen as players. The following summer Stephen Teal from Yeadon in Yorkshire replaced Stainton as leader. Teal remained until 1891 when he was succeeded by another Yorkshireman, Walter Atkinson from Sowerby Bridge, and under his baton the band won 29 national contests. This photograph may have been taken to celebrate the appointment of Robert Rimmer, from Southport in Lancashire, as the new leader in 1904. *Front row* (left to right): unknown; A. Beattie; J. Riddle; bowler-hatted Robert Rimmer; A. Simpson; unknown; W. Warwick; unknown. *Middle row*: W. Kirkpatrick (this drum still in use by the band); unknown; unknown; N. Walker; unknown; unknown; G. Scott; W. Hair; J. Anderson. *Back row*: unknown; unknown; unknown; H. Douglas; A.B. Scott; W. Riddle; J. Ballantyne; J. Scott. The band, with its 28 senior and fifteen junior members, is still going strong – what would the Common Riding or the Vertish Hill Sports be without it? Today, the only other known saxhorn bands in Britain are at Flimby in Cumbria and Dodworth in Yorkshire.

Hawick's Salvation Army Corps was founded in January 1887 by Captain Samuel Gainn from Hexham. Initially, they met in the Croft Street Temperance Hall, but when it was demolished to build Scott of Motherwell's Theatre Cinema (Scott's also ran the Pavilion Cinema in High Street and the Odeon), the Salvationists moved to Mill Path. It too, in turn, became run-down and derelict and the corps returned to Croft Street – this time based in their own building – in 1962. As this photograph of the band includes Captain William Boyd, it can be dated to sometime during his tenure as the commanding officer – 13 January 1921 to 18 May 1922. *Front row*: Tom Eston; Gilbert Oliver. *Middle row*: unknown; Robert Cairns; Mrs Capt. Boyd; Band Master Archie Elliot; Captain William Boyd; Alex Smith; William Mather. *Back row*: unknown; Stuart Waugh; William Mayo (knit-machine worker at Pringle); Standard Bearer Jimmy Richardson; John Smith; the Bass Drummer (name unknown); Tom Helm (who also played with Hawick Saxhorn Band); George Cairns; unknown; George Scott.

Hawick ex-Soldiers Association Pipe Band. Believed to have been founded in the early 1920s, as the Boy Scout Pipe Band led the 1919 Armistice parade, little information on this band survives, although Pipe Major Jimmy Hall is thought to be on the left of the group. Initially, they wore the Leslie tartan, but in acknowledgement of their first pipe major, C.E. Macdonald, they changed to the Macdonald tartan. They were disbanded in the mid 1950s.

Offering, perhaps, a different range of melodies, the itinerant 'Border Minstrel' Albert Wallace was well known from Langholm to Berwick. This photograph dates from 1906.

Why this group of pre-First World War pupils, photographed in their playground at Drumlanrig School, should consist only of girls (with three of their male teachers) is unknown. As a result of the 1867 Reform Act, extending the franchise to male adult householders and male lodgers paying over £10 annual rent, 1.5 million new voters were created – the children of whom the government thought should be educated. The Education (Scotland) Act 1872 divided the country into districts, each having an elected school board, and in a huge social shift, not only were women allowed to vote for these boards, they were also able to stand as candidates for them. Free education was now compulsory to the age of fourteen and new schools sprang up across the country. In Hawick the old Industrial, or 'Ragged', School became the new Drumlanrig Board School, opening in September 1873. This building, shown here, was demolished and replaced by Drumlanrig St Cuthbert's Primary School which opened on 1 September 1960.

A 1913 photograph of a teacher and pupils, possibly the nine year olds of class four, of the Episcopal School on Lynnwood Road in 1913. The school was opposite the Episcopal Church of St Cuthbert.

Edwardian pupils of St Mary's Infant School (for children of five to eight years old) on Brougham Place, with their headmistress, Miss Burnet.

The office bearers of Lodge St James No. 424, photographed by J.E.D. Murray (Past Master and Lodge Bard) on 16 November 1944. *Front row* (left to right): J.C. Hogarth; Edward S. Lyon; John S. Bett; J. Wallace; John Lees. *Middle row*: David Irvine; John Cook; W. Blacklock; James Hope; R.H. Broatch. *Back row*: G. Dalgleish; John Johnstone; W. Elliot; G. Lyle. Having 'for some time past kept up a Brotherly Society of Masons without any regular constitution', Hawick was granted a charter by the Grand Lodge of Scotland on 15 March 1768 and became Lodge St John, No. 111. It became dormant in the late 1830s, but resumed in 1860. Following a split two years later, a breakaway faction was granted a charter and formed Lodge No. 424.

Having served with the King's Own Scottish Borderers, these men were 'seeing out' their three-and-a-half years with the Territorials at Hawick before full demobilisation. Photographed in the Drill Hall in Dovecot Street in the early 1950s, the following have been recognised – *standing* (from left to right): Tommy Walton; Bertie Robson; Robert Marshall; John Murphy; Graham Elliot; Jim Tait; Jim Anderson; Tom Moffat; Tom Maybin; unknown; unknown; George Currie; Bill Potter. *Seated*: unknown; Tony Murray; George Amos; unknown; James Nichol; unknown; George Marshall; Ian Anderson.

Three Edwardian ladies and a girl, tending what is thought to be a sale of work in aid of St Cuthbert's Church.

Roller Skating Carnival 30th Jany 1917

Four of the participants in the fund-raising Roller Skating Carnival, organised by Mr C.W. Grieve of Branxholme Park and held in the Exchange Hall Rink on 30 January 1917. The event attracted over 100 skaters, many in fancy dress, and the evening raised over £20 in aid of the Red Cross, the Scottish Women's Hospital, the King's Own Scottish Borderers and the families of prisoners of war. Those in the photograph cannot be identified, but second from the right may be Miss Hogg who won the 'Ladies' Prettiest Costume' class. A Miss Chalmers, appearing as a 'cow girl', was judged to have the most original costume.

A coalman on his rounds at the end of Needle Street around 1910, when coal was 8½d per cwt sack. As the cart bears no name, we cannot know which of the eight Hawick coalmen it belonged to. At the time there was George Blaikie and the Co-op in High Street, Robson and Eckford & Co. and Maben at the railway station, Cranstone on Mansfield Road, Adam Hart of Lockieshedge in Wilton, Drummond in Trinity Street, and Thomas Rutherford in Wellogate Place.

A cart, possibly from J. Cairncross & Co. of Kirk Wynd, delivering to Agnew the confectioner's shop in Myreslawgreen around 1907. The firm of Cairncross specialised in bottled aerated water from their own artesian well and brewed ginger beer.

At the wheel of a new Albion A lorry around 1906 is John Rae of J. Rae & Sons, the builders and plumbers who were based on Victoria Road. On the platform with the dogs may be his father, John senior. Young John was Cornet in 1923, which saw the wettest Common Riding in living memory and gave rise to doubts about the wisdom of choosing a plumber!

Commemorated by a public subscription statue in Wilton Lodge Park in 1939, Jimmie Guthrie, 'Hawick's Racing Legend' and the greatest motorcycle rider of his time, was killed in the 500cc, 40-lap, 346-kilometre Germany Grand Prix at Sachsenring on 8 August 1937, aged just 40. Having that year already won the Belgian and Swiss Grand Prix he was favourite to win, and having lapped all the others but one, Karl Gall (BMW), the Union Jack was being attached to the flag pole in the last seconds awaiting his appearance out of the final bend. Instead, Gall took the chequered flag, having passed the fatally injured Guthrie at the trackside. This photograph celebrates his success in the Isle of Man Senior (500cc) Race the previous year.

A promotional postcard, sent to a Miss Walker at Redfordgreen Farm, for Buffalo Bill's Wild West Exhibition and Congress of Rough Riders of the World which opened its 1904 24-venue Scottish tour at Hawick's Whitlaw Haugh on Tuesday, 26 July. Arriving at the railway station at 5.00 a.m., three special trains disgorged 800 staff and 500 horses, plus equipment. The company then paraded through cheering crowds to the showground, where everything was set and ready by 7.30 a.m. There were two performances – one at 2.00 p.m. which attracted 4 to 5,000, and one at 8.00 p.m. for a crowd of 10,000. The show opened with the Rough Riders of the World, led by a band of whooping Indians, dashing breakneck into the arena, rending the air with the thunder of hoofs and the clash of arms. The Indians, the *Hawick Express* reported, were 'big muscular men with jet black hair streaming in the breeze, almost all in their primitive habit, their naked skins being coloured and crossed with all the designs of savagery'. This was followed by a reproduction of the Battle of the Little Big Horn, a hold-up of the 'Deadwood Stage' by redskins, who were routed, a Mexican display of lassoing, Indian attacks on a wagon train crossing the prairie (the Indians were repulsed by scouts), military drills by veteran cavalrymen of Great Britain and Japan (referred to in the report as the 'elusive little Jap'), and acrobatic feats by Arab horsemen. There was then a display of marksmanship by Colonel William F. Cody himself. It must have been 'the talk of the town' for weeks afterwards.

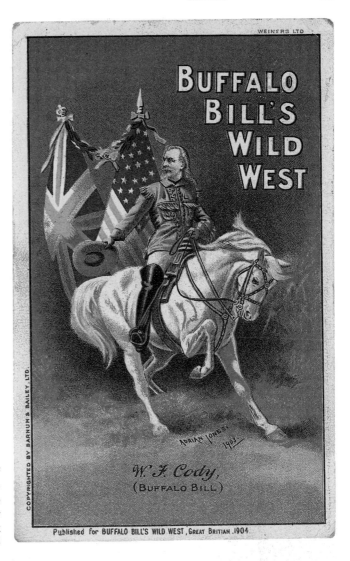

The reverse of the postcard to Miss Walker, signed 'Cody', was posted at Hawick for the 10.45 p.m. uplift on the day of his visit. It is not known how they came to be in communication, or how he found the time to remember her (possibly the signature was faked!). Amongst the 800 people with the show were doctors and vets and 25 bonesetters. Each day it took three butchers, ten cooks and 25 carvers to prepare the 25 cwt of meat (sent each day from a supplier in Birkenhead to wherever the show was performing), 1400 lbs of vegetables, 800 lbs of potatoes and 600 loaves eaten by the company, and 28 waiters to serve all of it. The 500 horses got through 600 bushels of corn and six tons of hay. And, 24 hours after arriving in Hawick, they were arriving at Galashiels, and the day after at Motherwell, and the day after that at Coatbridge, then Dumbarton and Glasgow (which had been the only Scottish venue on the 1891/92 British tour). The final Scottish show in 1904 was at Cresswell Park at Dumfries on 14 September.

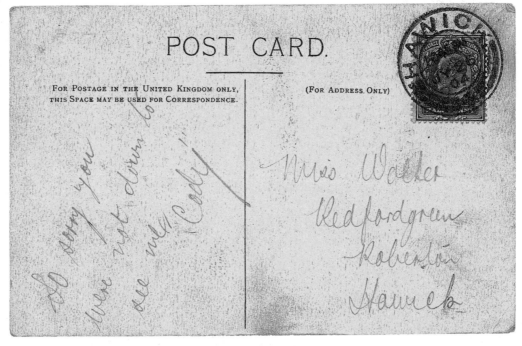

A procession of children passes from the Square along High Street, on its way to the annual sports at Vertish Hill around 1909. The premises along their route were, from right to left (starting at No. 64), the Half Moon Hotel (proprietor, William Park), the grocers Borthwick Turnbull & Co., Mrs Wilson's china shop, the Glencairn Bar, Rule, the tobacconist, and the tailors Kerr & McKenzie.

On the last Saturday in June, Hawick Golf Club (founded 1877) gives up its 5,933-yard, eighteen-hole, par-69 parkland course for the Vertish Hill Sports Day. Starting in 1881 as a kite-flying competition, the day developed into a sports day for children, attracting for the 1897 Jubilee a crowd of 12,000.

The jockey Mr Webb on Mr Joseph's horse Fasola and pictured after winning the 1913 seven-furlong Tradesmen's Handicap (and a purse of 46 sovereigns) at odds of five to one against, in a field of seven. The favourite at two to one against, Revenge, ridden by Mr Thornton, came fifth. Fasola led from the start and won by almost two lengths. In the Municipal Handicap race, Webb came third on Mr Joseph's Teribus, and was fined £2.2s for disobedience at the post. He was also reported to the stewards of the British Racing Club and was not allowed to ride again until the fine was paid.

Hawick Race Meeting on Friday, 11 June 1910, where the bookmakers, Mr Dick, Fred Galletta and Reginald West, all of Edinburgh, are fairing better in the minutes before the Tradesmen's Handicap, won by the horse Fasola, than the ice cream vendor Henry Barrie. Standing to the left of his round-topped board, in shirt sleeves and waistcoat, above the two white parasols towards the left of the picture, is 32-year-old Fred Galletta. A master hairdresser, Fred had days out from his barber shop in Leith's Henderson Street to work at the point-to-point race meetings in the Borders. He died in May 1948. This scene of a pleasant and relaxed afternoon is, if the press were to be believed, deceptive, for amongst the crowd were 'the usual influx of questionable characters who are in the habit of frequenting race meetings'.

HAWICK RACES, 1910. R.C. NO. 19.

The Hawick Common Riding of 1907 may have brought a record number of showmen to the Haugh, but, as the *Hawick Advertiser* reported, the changeable weather 'seriously interfered with business'. This show – offering upwards of 50 novelties, from a 'Flying Fox' to the 'Tasmanian Devil', and all for a penny – cannot be identified despite its

spectacular frontage. However, by this time traditional shows such as this were being eclipsed by modern attractions like Wilson's Cinematograph Show, Biddall's Moving Pictures, Green's Bioscope, Miller's Living Pictures and John Cottrell's Electric Theatre, all of which were also competing for business that year.

Another view of the showground from 1907. As can be seen from the puddles and buckets, it was a very wet week. Under the shadow of the helter skelter, the avenue is lined with sideshows and stalls, the first three on the left being shooting galleries. On the right, beyond the man wringing something out, is Macintosh's double stall which specialised in shies. Their variant on the 'cokernut' (coconut) shy had celebrity heads in the cups and for many years – certainly in the era of this photograph – the favourite targets were Boer War generals.

The 1907 Cornet Thomas Jardine 'dipping the flag' at Spetchman's Haugh. He is flanked by Right Hand Man J.W.S. Robertson, spirit merchant and the Cornet of 1906, and Left Hand Man, William E. Kyle, the Cornet of 1905. This tradition involves lowering the staff of the standard into the water three times to mark the town's boundary. In the background is the mill of Innes, Henderson's Knitwear Co., demolished in March 2004.

Chief Constable David Thom leads Cornet Andrew Douglas Haddon and the procession along High Street on its way to the Moor in 1910. The Burgh Police (Scotland) Act of 1833 empowered Scottish burgh councils to establish a body of police commissioners within councils that could form their own police forces. Hawick's commissioners were formed in late 1845 and the new force, Hawick Burgh Police, consisting of a superintendent and five constables, appeared on the streets of the town on 26 May 1846. Constables and superintendents came and went, some good and some not so good. In his summation at a trial at the 1861 Jedburgh Spring Circuit Court, for a murder in Hawick, the Lord Justice Clerk said, 'I have been impressed with the strong conviction that the police force in the town of Hawick is by no means what it ought to be'. Presumably, things improved. In 1902 the idea of amalgamating the force with Roxburghshire County Police was mooted but dismissed. However, amalgamation with the county force came in 1930 with the implementation of the Local Government (Scotland) Act 1929.

The 1910 Cornet, A. Douglas Haddon, along with Right Hand Man Thomas Scott (Cornet, 1909), Left Hand Man James Glendinning (Cornet ,1908) and Acting Father James Conn, 'Singing the Song' at Pilmuir. Born in Kilmarnock, Ayrshire, 39-year-old Conn was a solicitor with Haddon & Turnbull at the Royal Bank Buildings in High Street and also Hawick's Burgh Chamberlain. Third from the left, with the riding whip in his hand, is Sir John Nicholson Barron (1872–1952) of Sawley Hall, Ripon, Yorkshire, Liberal MP for Hawick Burghs from 1909 to 1918.

Holding fast the 'Blue Banner', Cornet W.L. Thorburn makes the 'Chase' up the Nipknowes to Pilmuir for the 'Curds and Cream' on Common Riding morning, 1911. That year the Callants built the cairn at the Auld Ca' Knowe, marking the spot where the Roll is called.

A 'hurdy-gurdy', or barrel organ, at the 1913 Common Riding and carrying a photograph of that year's Cornet, Robert Elder. The Saxhorn Band players may have been there to admire his music – or to keep him right!

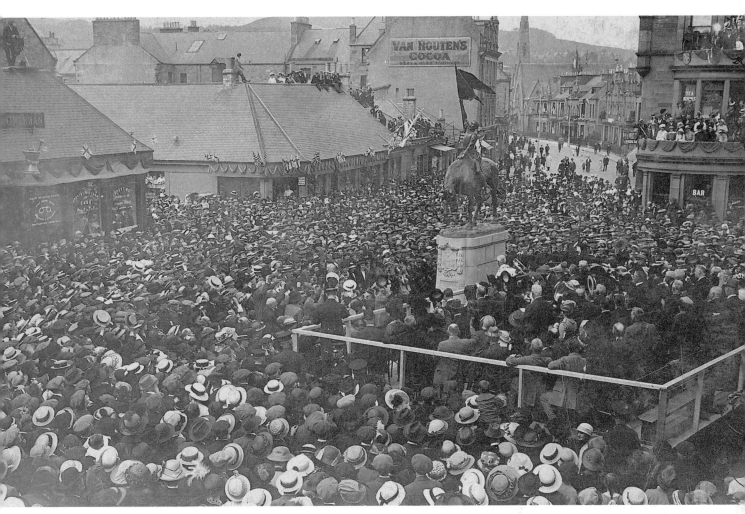

The afternoon of Thursday 4 June 1914 brought the highlight of the quater-centenary celebrations – the unveiling of the Horse Memorial in Central Square by Lady Sybil Scott (1899–1990), younger daughter of the Earl of Dalkeith. The memorial celebrates the Hawick Callants' 1514-rout of marauding Englishmen at Hornshole and the capture of the Hexham Pennant. From a public subscription fund exceeding £1,440 (the aspiration of the fund reaching £1,514 was not realised), the work was executed by the Hawick-born, Edinburgh-based sculptor, William Francis Beattie. He served in the First World War as a major with the 73rd Battery of the 5th Brigade of the Royal Field Artillery and was killed in action on 3 October 1918.

The platform of officials and guests at the unveiling of the Horse Memorial. The Saxhorn Band are on the left and in front of the officials is a table for the press.

Part of the crowd in front of the platform at the unveiling of the Horse Memorial.

The town's quater-centenary celebrations, during the 1914 Common Riding week, opened on Friday 29 May with a civic reception for overseas visitors. This was followed by the Vertish Hill Sports on the Saturday, a service at St Mary's Church on the Sunday, and a Grand Historical Pageant in Volunteer Park on the Tuesday and Wednesday evenings. This photograph shows Miss Margot Barclay, 'Queen of the Borderland' – the pageant's central figure – circling the park in her 'Car of State' which was drawn by 21 'boy pages'. On this occasion these included Jackie Sim, Jackie Amos, Robert Domingo, Balfour Thomline and Tom Laidlaw. The proceedings had opened with a fanfare of trumpets and the entrance of the Heralds – Messrs Dryden and Thompson, Walter Montgomery, Joseph Halley, Melgund Murray and J. McQueen. They were followed by Father Time (Mr J.M. Morrison) and his 29 daughters, representing spring, summer, autumn, winter, Spirits of the Night, Spirits of the Dawn, and the Harbinger of Sunrise. The evening closed with the singing of 'Hail Borderland'.

Watched by the Halbardier, the Burgh Officer Tom Waldie, the Principals of the 1919 Common Riding dance the Cornet's Reel at the Friday's games in Volunteer Park. From the left are Right Hand Man George Wilson (Cornet, 1914), Left Hand Man Robert Elder (Cornet, 1913), Acting Father C.W. Grieve, and that year's Cornet Tom G. Winning. This first Common Riding following the First World War was as much about the memory of those the town had lost as it was a celebration. Cornet Winning, a partner with the solicitors Guthrie & Winning in High Street, had served in the war. He had been a trooper with the Lothians and Berwickshire Imperial Yeomanry from 1905 to 1908 and, on the outbreak of war, had joined the Lothians and Border Horse, serving in Salonika and Egypt.

Cornet John C.G. Landles, with Right Hand Man Robert E. Tait (Cornet, 1920), Left Hand Man Thomas G. Winning (Cornet, 1919) and Acting Father, 41-year-old Lieutenant Colonel John Gould Kennedy, MC, DSO (later OBE), follow the fifes and drums through Drumlanrig Square on their way to the Moor during the 1921 Common Riding. A real 'Teri' (a native of Hawick), born in the Sandbed, John Chapman Gray Landles was the son of Bailie Andrew Landles of Sunnybrae, Langlands Road. Back in Hawick as a hosiery worker, and player with Hawick Waverley football team, he had been demobbed on the eve of the 1919 Common Riding, having spent the war with the Lothians and Border Horse and the 1st Battalion, Royal Scots, in Salonika, Serbia and Russia. In 1927 he married Elizabeth Wingate Inglis, and following his father's footsteps, was elected to both Hawick Burgh Council and Roxburghshire Council in 1930.

Cornet James E. Glenny, with Right Hand Man Thomas P. Alison (1926 Cornet and son of architect James P. Alison) and Left Hand Man G.D. Scott (Cornet, 1925), approaching the Rev. Rodgie's (1777–1861) 'Old Green Kirk' in Myreslawgreen to partake of the Stirrup Cup on the Saturday afternoon of the Common Riding, 1927. In Rodgie's day the Kirk, or 1st United Secession Church, stood off the Green Wynd and was surrounded by fields.

Part of the 1931 'Friday morning' motorcade, approaching Tower Knowe, on its way to the Moor. In the lead car, an early 1920s Sunbeam Landaulette, are the Lassies, followed by an Albion charabanc with Provost David Fisher and the town council. The horse-drawn carriage contained the Common Riding committee. That year's Cornet was A R. Innes.

A Cornet coming down Albert Road, making for Princes Street, in the 1920s. This photograph was taken during the ceremony of marking the boundaries. On the left is Scoon & Hood's Mill and on the right the Albert Mills. All of this area has since been swept away and replaced by the area around Wilton Path.

The Hawick Ba' of 1906. A traditional Borders game associated with Shrove Tuesday, and possibly originating in Jedburgh, the first Hawick Ba' was played in 1842 and remained an annual event until the Second World War. Played in and around Commercial Road and the river, the contenders were the West Enders and the East Enders, each trying to land the ball in the others 'hail'. The original hails were the toll bar at the Haugh end of Commercial Road and the old town boundary opposite Dickson's & Laing's mill, but they changed in the 1850s to the Cobble Cauld and the railway bridge. There could be up to six games on the day. The uninitiated may have thought it nothing more than a melee – one year, part of the game was played over roofs in the Sandbed – and it could be dangerous as there were injuries and even drownings.

Hawick-born Thomas E. Crosby, the 1950 Cornet, had his working life in the liquor trade interrupted by the Second World War, during which he served in the Royal Air Force. Later, he took to mink farming until the trade in animal pelts went into decline. Prior to his early death in the 1980s, he worked for the knitwear manufacturer George Hogg & Sons.

Grace Miller, the 1950 Cornet's Lass, was a hairdresser at George Scott's Imperial Salon. She later married an Indian-tea planter, Tom Elliot, and moved to the subcontinent. On their retiral from the business they came back to live in Berwickshire.

This photograph of 'Hawick Common Riding in Middelburg, Cape Colony' appeared on a postcard that was sent to Miss Marion Walker at West Redfordgreen Farm from Kimberley, South Africa, on 13 July 1903. None of the men pictured are known, but it is possible that one or more of the men were emigrants from Hawick or Roxburghshire. Marion Walker was then a 23 year old.

A pre-hunt gathering of grooms, awaiting their masters due for the Duke of Buccleuch's Hunt, in the hamlet of Appletreehall in the 1920s. It was also a busy time for the blacksmith or

farrier. On the left is the whitewashed Appletreehall House. Now virtually a dormitory village of Hawick, Appletreehall once had a water-driven wool-spinning mill and, by the late nineteenth century, provided business for two blacksmiths, two masons, a master carpenter, a road contractor and a veterinary surgeon.

The monument on Denholm's green was raised in 1861 to commemorate the village's most famous son, the poet and orientalist Dr John Leyden. Born on 8 September 1775, he studied for the ministry at Edinburgh University and in 1798 was licensed as a preacher by the presbytery of St Andrews. He assisted Sir Walter Scott, collecting traditional ballads for his 1803 publication, *Minstrelsey of the Scottish Border.* That same year, having gained a medical qualification, Leyden sailed for Madras, ostensibly as an assistant surgeon to the hospital there, but more likely to further his interest in languages. He is said to have acquired 34 and he translated the Gospels into five of them. In 1811 he accompanied Sir Gilbert Elliot Minto (1751–1814), Governor General of India (1807–1813), on an expedition to Java in the East Indies, where, working in a library in Batavia (now Jakarta), he contracted 'Batavian Fever' and died within three days, on 28 August 1811. Although Leyden's genius was recognised in his lifetime, it wasn't until 1859 that a committee was formed in his home village to raise a monument to his memory. Following the demolition of the school on the green, work began in May 1861, using stone from the Swinton sandstone quarry in Berwickshire (also used for the 1927 National War Memorial at Edinburgh Castle) and granite from Peterhead. The monument was unveiled in October 1861 by Sir William Scott of Ancrum, then MP for Roxburghshire.

Main Street in the summer of 1909.

The Canongate in the early 1900s.

The Eastgate, or 'Butcher's Corner', with Thomas Beattie's shop to the right, at the end of Main Street, and Eastgate House in the distance, beyond the white palisade fence.

Westside from the Main Street corner with Wester Green, Haddon House, Rae Cottage and Barries Cottage along the left side. On the Sunnyside corner, in the centre of the photograph, is the school which was built in 1858 on land gifted by James Douglas of Cavers. This replaced the school on the green, which had been demolished for the Leyden monument, and was later to become the village hall. At the time of this 1908 photograph, the schoolmaster was 51-year-old Andrew Oliver, who had come from Caver's Cogsmill School with his widowed sister, Margaret Irvine, who taught sewing.

The Westgate, looking to the Green, with the seventeenth-century Westgate Hall, thought to be the oldest surviving building in the village, on the left. Around 1903 the upper floor was given to the village by Captain Edward Palmer Douglas of Midgard for use as a hall. For access to this the outside stairway, seen here just after its completion, was built. Painters are busy working on the Co-op dairy opposite.

The Denholm Co-operative Dairy Society's premises in Westgate, photographed around 1906. It had no connection with the national 'Co-op', but is reckoned to have been established in the late nineteenth century and was being run by George Watson of Rillbank by the early twentieth century. Although it opened a branch in Hawick, it appears to have closed after the First World War. The 'bus', despite its conductor with his bell punch ticket machine, was actually a lorry, built at Arrol Johnston's Underwood Works, Paisley, in 1904. If it was a Cairns & Welsh bus then it may have been owned by George Cairns, the timber merchant of Denholm Sawmill.

Thornbank was worked as a farm by the Barrie brothers until the late nineteenth century, but by the time of this photograph – the summer of 1904 – it had become a dwelling house. The woman on the right is Miss Catherine Dalgleish Ormiston, then 50 years old. Through Haddon and Turnbull the Hawick solicitors, she held life rental of the property until her death on 17 January 1930. She appears in the 1881 census as Catherine Ormiston, born at Bowden, near Melrose, and at that time an unmarried 27-year-old general servant to the Barrie family at Greenhead Farm House, Selkirk. In the old parochial register for Bowden she is listed as Catharine Ormiston, born 18 March 1854 to James Ormiston and Mary Dalgleish who had married at Traquair on 8 December 1844.

A Denholm Choir picnic at Furniehirst Castle in the early 1900s – when the sopranos outnumbered the tenors. Little can be found on the choir's history or repertoire, but the fifteenth-century castle has a well documented history. Standing by the Jed Water, south of Jedburgh, it was built in 1476 by Sir Thomas Kerr, but was attacked and seized by the English in 1523. It was retaken in 1549, only to be recaptured by the English in 1570. Rebuilt in 1598, it was habitable until around 1800 when it fell into decay.

Mr W.M. Price of Cleughhead, factor to Minto Estate, driving the first stroke at the opening of the four-hole Denholm Golf Course in July 1907. To the left, in the dark suit, is Mr Douglas Oliver of Hassendeanbank. Laid out at the top of Ashloaning, the course was used until at least the First World War, and was superseded by the current Minto Golf Course which opened in 1928.

The tower-house known as Fatlips Castle on Minto Craigs (or 'Mantoncrake' or 'Mynto Crag') in the 1920s, before its days of neglect. Built by the Turnbulls of Barnhills in the sixteenth century, its commanding position (729 feet above sea level) marked it out as a conspicuous landmark over a wide area. It was bought by Sir Gilbert Elliot of Minto in 1705 and his family carried out two restorations – firstly in 1857 when the freestone dressings were replaced, and again in 1897/98 under the direction of the architect Sir Robert Lorimer. The latter work included the addition of a shooting box and, inside, a museum. According to the Borders writer and publisher Robert Chambers (1802–71) its name derives from the tradition that 'every gentleman, by indefeasible privilege, kisses one of the ladies on entering the ruin'. A more prosaic explanation of the name derives from the trait of full lips among members of the Turnbull family.

To a design by the London-born, Edinburgh-based architect, William Henry Playfair (1789–1857), the 360-seat, Gothic-style Minto Parish Church, along with the Tuscan-style manse, was built of local stone in 1831. Playfair's Edinburgh works included the Royal Scottish Academy, the National Gallery of Scotland, the Royal College of Surgeons and the National Monument on Calton Hill. The schoolhouse can be seen to the left.

Minto School in the early twentieth century. In the first *Statistical Account* of Minto Parish (1799), the Rev. William Burn reports there being only one schoolmaster in the parish, who had a house, a garden, a schoolhouse, between 50 and 60 scholars, and a salary of £12. So small and confined was the original school that in March 1792 over 50 pupils caught the measles in two days. The heritors found an airy location for the new school – 'the most beautiful and commodious in the south of Scotland' – and by 1838 the roll had risen to 112 and the teacher's salary to £100. By 1883 the roll was down to 69, with the average attendance at 29. The building in the photograph bears the date 1889, but with an ever-decreasing roll it closed in the 1950s and by the 1970s had been converted into a dwelling house.

Lord and Lady Minto, with their daughters, Lady Eileen (on the left), Lady Ruby (sitting) and Lady Violet, at Minto House around 1910. The house was built in 1813 from designs by Archibald Elliot. Born in 1845, Gilbert John Elliot-Murray-Kynynmond married Mary Caroline Grey, daughter of Sir Charles Grey, secretary to Queen Victoria, in July 1883. Their eldest daughter, Eileen Nina Evelyn Sibell, (1884–1938), married Lord Francis George Montagu-Douglas-Scott, the sixth son of the 6th Duke of Buccleuch in 1915. In 1908, Ruby Florence Mary (1886–1961) became wife to the 2nd Earl of Cromer. Violet Mary (1889–1965) went on to spend most of her life in south-east England, serving as a county councillor for Kent (1946–51), and was granted the freedom of Dover. In January 1909 she married Lord Charles George Francis Mercer Nairne, younger son of the 5th Marquis of Lansdowne. Francis, a major attached to the 6th Cavalry Brigade, was killed at Ypres on 30 October 1914. In August 1916 she married Lieutenant Colonel John Jacob Astor, 1st Baron Astor of Hever, and she died in January 1965. The house is now derelict.

The gateway to Minto House festooned with flags, bunting and garlands welcoming the return of Lord and Lady Minto. But where were they returning from? Following a career in the military as a private secretary, military secretary or *aide-de-camp* to commanders in Afghanistan, Cape Colony, Egypt and Canada, Lord Minto was appointed Governor General of Canada in

November 1898 and served in this post until December 1904 when he was succeeded by Lady Minto's brother, Earl Grey. The following year, 1905, he was made Viceroy of India, following the resignation of Lord Curzon, with Lady Minto becoming the Vicereine. The welcome then may have been for their return from Canada in 1904 or their homecoming from India in 1910.

Pupils from Minto Public School, along with Boy Scouts from Hawick and possibly Denholm, line the roadside awaiting Lord

Minto's funeral cortege on its way from Minto House to the church on Wednesday, 4 March 1914.

Lord Minto's funeral cortege passing Minto School on its way to the family burial ground in Minto churchyard. Following a noon service in the great hall at Minto House, conducted by the Rev. Lancelot Andrewes, chaplain to the Duke of Buccleuch, the Union Jack draped coffin, on which rested the late Earl's sword and military cap, was placed on a gun carriage drawn by six horses from the 1st Brigade, Royal Field Artillery. The procession then set off, led by Pipe-Major Ross of the Scots Guards playing 'The Flowers of the Forest'.

In his report on the six-square-mile parish of Bedrule for the *New Statistical Account* (1845), the Rev. Archibald Craig wrote of a once populous parish having dwindled away. However, in the village of Bedrule itself the houses were '. . . all lately built, and being covered with slate . . . have a very neat and cheerful appearance.' He also reported that '. . . the commodious farmhouse of Mr [Robert] Brodie [of Nottylees] is partly new ' The Barony of Bedrule was bought by William Elliot of Wells in 1801, and on his death in 1818 it passed to Sir William Elliot of Stobs. In 1896 Elliot sold the Wells Estate, with Bedrule and Fulton, to Sir Robert Usher of Norton, Midlothian (1860–1933). This photograph from around 1910 shows the farmhouse and the terrace of cottages stretching beyond. The tenant farmer between 1898 and 1921, living in the 'commodious farmhouse', was Thomas Aird Smith, and the houses were occupied by William Oliver, a steward, John Wemyss, a ploughman, Andrew Davidson, a shepherd, John Notman, a groom, John Foster, a ploughman of minor age, and Thomas Dalgleish, a byreman.

The village in the early 1920s, as viewed from the Hawick road which runs down over the Rule Water bridge. The four-house terrace on the left and the Bridge Inn opposite it on the right are just discernible through the trees. Also through the branches can be seen the charabanc of the public carrier Henry Anderson, parked outside his house. Earlier, he had operated a horse and cart. From these early beginnings came the transport firm Thomas Anderson & Son, which celebrated its centenary in 1981.

Many years have passed since the three large trees on the right were felled. For a time they were replaced by petrol pumps, but these too have gone. On the left is the Bridge Inn (now the Horse and Hound) and the premises of Henderson the saddler.

Opened in September 1899, funds for the William Laidlaw Memorial Hall were left to Bonchester by William Laidlaw of the 210-acre Easter Fodderlie Farm, to the north east of the village. He had died in May 1884, aged 68. This photograph was taken around 1911. The hall was managed by a board of trustees, chaired at this time by schoolmaster Thomas Culbertson of Hobkirk, and consisted of the ground-floor public rooms, a hall, a kitchen, a cloakroom, and an upstairs residence for the caretaker – a position then occupied by a widow, Mrs Margaret Smith. Still the venue for local events, the trustees received a Lottery Community Fund grant of £95,000 in November 2002 for much-needed renovation work.

An Edwardian fund-raising 'Costermonger's Fair' at Bonchester, held in aid of Roxburghshire Nursing Association and Hobkirk Nursing Fund. Seated on her cart, whip in hand, is Lady Eileen Elliot, daughter of Lord Minto and winner of the 'best and most original Coster's Cart' competition.

Standing on the Jedburgh road, Weens Cottages, or 'Sclaintie Cottages', were owned by James Tancred of Weens House at the time of this 1908 photograph. On the left is the shop and house of the boot-and-shoe merchant and tobacconist James W. Mutch, then 63 years old. Taking over the lease on Whitsunday 1884, he and his wife Jessie had moved from 9 Lothian Road, Hawick. In the middle house lived the Melrose-born postman Robert Thomson and his wife, Mary. To the right is the post office.

Bonchester Post Office opened in 1836 and this is perhaps the postmistress of the early 1900s, Miss Margaret Sibbald (born 26 October 1845). In the days when her father William had been postmaster, Margaret had assisted him as clerk. She was also clerk to the school board.

Three quarters of a mile south of Bonchester Bridge, Hobkirk, or Hopekirk (a 'hope' being a small valley or glen opening into a larger valley), is a small community based around the parish church and school. The church dates from 1858 (restored in 1914), when it was built to replace the old kirk of 1692. In the parish's entry in the *New Statistical Account*, written in March 1836, the Rev. John Ewen comments that although the old church was 'centrically [*sic*] placed', it was 'a considerable distance from the extremities of the parish'. In 1741 a belfry was added, but the church remained heather thatched until 1777 when it was slated. In the photograph, under the shadow of the church, stands the original, 148-pupil school. This has been a dwelling house since the opening of the new school in 1937. Against the wall of the shelter at the rear, is a mounting block, catering for children who arrived on ponies. In its walled garden to the left is the schoolmaster's house, and to the right is Hartshaugh Mill Farm.

Competitors at the 1906 Hobkirk Games. With the cross pencilled across his chest is Thomson (first name unknown) of St Boswells, who won the Handicap Race, and second from the right, with the pipe, is thought to be Billy Scott from Wolfehopelee.

Hislop the blacksmith's shop on the crossroads at Chesters in Southdean Parish around 1906. Standing in the house doorway is Agnes Hislop (whose father had been blacksmith at Fountainhall) with her son Robert. Her Duns-born husband, Alexander, is by the other doorway. The young fellow amongst the ploughs would have been his apprentice. Arriving in 1904, with Agnes, his 31-year-old wife, Alex (then 33 years old) not only worked the smiddy in Chesters, but had a weekly trip to work at Catclough, across the Carter Bar. They ran the smiddy until the late 1940s when Alex, then in his late 70s, sold the business to Jim Falla of Bonchester Bridge. The babe in arms, Robert, followed his father's trade but was tragically killed when he fell from a roof in 1937. The house beyond, at the left of the photograph, belonged to Sibbald the joiner.

John Wilson's Register of Deaths for Hawick (1825–1862) records the passing of Gilbert Aitken of Adderstonshiels on 3 May 1832. The records are then silent until the arrival at the farm of John Davidson and his wife, Annie, in the late 1850s. The census return of 1881 records the Davidsons as occupiers of the 1,300-acre farm (375 of them arable), along with their dairymaid, Jemima McGlasson from Canonbie in Dumfriesshire, and Jane Little, a general servant from England. It also records their children: Margaret Armstrong Davidson (b. 1858), Andrew Davidson (b. 1860, an apprentice draper), Gilbert Davidson, (b. 1861, an apprentice law clerk), Annie Stavert Davidson (b. 1865, a scholar), and John Davidson (b. 1869, a scholar), who succeeded his father on the farm. This photograph from 1908 shows the front of the farmhouse with, it is thought, John Davidson Junior's five-year-old son, another John, on the farm donkey. He, in turn, succeeded to the farm which he worked until his death in 1977. The 'Victorian Ropetop' edging survives, and the Monkey Puzzle tree is now taller than the house.

Photographed in the 1920s is William Thomson, flanked by his wife Jane and daughter Elizabeth, in the garden of their cottage at Adderstonshiels Farm, where William was a ploughman. He died in November 1942, aged 76, and Jane (maiden name Cowan) died in December 1944, aged 79. They had three children: John (see the picture on page 20), Helen, and Elizabeth who – having lost her sweetheart in the First World War – remained unmarried. For many years she was housekeeper to Dr David A.R. Haddon at 19 Buccleuch Street, Hawick. She died in August 1981 and was buried in her parents' grave at Cavers churchyard.

The Edinburgh-born architect Robert Adam (1728–92) died before completing the building of the picturesquely situated Stobs Castle for the Elliots. A 'castle-style mini-mansion', it contained four public rooms, twelve bedrooms (two with dressing rooms), a four-bedroom servants' quarter and ancillary accommodation. Advertised for sale as a 16,450-acre – including Hallrule and Lymiecleuch – 'sporting and residential estate near Hawick' in 1902, it was bought by the War Department as a training area. The castle served as an administration centre.

The postmaster at Stobs Camp Post Office, photographed by the professional photographer, J.P. Couper of St Vincent Street, Glasgow, around 1913/14. On the wall behind the postmaster, who, possibly due to his false beard, has not been recognised, is a calendar from David D. Deans, the fishing tackle merchant in Hawick's Oliver Place who also stocked and supplied guns, rifles, revolvers and ammunition. Although troops were issued with rifles and ammunition, in a society then virtually free of gun control, officers usually bought their own revolvers and ammunition.

According to the Postmaster General's Minute Books, Stobs Camp Post Office opened on 5 May 1911, as a sub-office of Hawick, and closed on 21 March 1915 when Stobs became a prisoner-of-war camp. However, this photograph of the postmaster and his assistant with a group of 'regimental postmen' setting out with satchels of mail for their respective regiments, comes from a card franked at Hawick on 16 July 1905.

Men of the Army Service Corps outside the YMCA refreshment tent. The photograph is undated but by 1907 the YMCA and Church of Scotland had moved into their newly built huts at the camp. The forerunners of today's Royal Logistic Corps, the Service Corps was responsible for the supply and transportation of troops and equipment. In 1918, by royal warrant, it became the Royal Army Service Corps.

A 'butcher's' shop in the early days at Stobs Camp when the War Department would have contracted local butchers to supply meat to detachments.

Each detachment at the camp had its own 'cookhouse'.